COMPASSION, JUSTICE
AND THE
CHRISTIAN
RETHINKING MINISTRY
TO THE POOR
LIFE

ROBERT D. LUPTON

BakerBooks

a division of Baker Publishing Group
Grand Rapids, Michigan

Published by Baker Books
a division of Baker Publishing Group
P.O. Box 6287, Grand Rapids, MI 49516-6287
www.bakerbooks.com

Baker Books edition published 2014
ISBN 978-0-8010-1791-9

Previously published by Regal Books

Originally published as *And You Call Yourself a Christian*.

Printed in the United States of America

The Library of Congress has cataloged the original edition as follows:
   Lupton, Robert D.
      Compassion, justice, and the Christian life / Robert D. Lupton.
         p. cm.
      ISBN 0-8307-4379-0 (trade paper)
         1. Community development—Religious aspects—Christianity. 2. Church work with the poor—United States. 3. Community development—United States. 4. City churches—United States. 5. City missions—United States. I. Title.
   BV625.L86   2007
   253'.09173'2—dc22   2006101230

14   15   16   17   18   19   20   7   6   5   4   3   2   1

*This book was made possible
because of Howard and Roberta Ahmanson's
long-term support for CCDA.*

CONTENTS

PART III
TOWARD RESPONSIBLE CHARITY

PART IV
FINAL THOUGHTS

FOREWORD

I have been proud to call Bob Lupton a friend for a number of years. Bob has been engaged in Christian community development for more than three decades in his native city of Atlanta, Georgia. And he has walked the walk as well as talked the talk.

He and his family have lived in the inner city neighborhoods that he has worked so faithfully and tirelessly to help redevelop.

In these pages, Bob shares what he has learned—some of it the hard way, as he will tell you—about the strategies, tactics and convictions needed for successful Christian community development. And his principles are based solidly in his belief in the authority of the Bible.

I can think of no better person to be writing about the subject of community development from a Christian perspective than Bob Lupton. And I think that as you read this book, you will agree.

John Perkins
President, John M. Perkins Foundation
and CCDA Chair Emeritus

PREFACE

The urban landscape is rapidly changing. Not long ago, the inner city was considered the wasteland for the disenfranchised. Not any longer, though. Long-neglected communities are now being rediscovered as rich new development opportunities. When the veteran founders of the Christian Community Development Association first advanced the bold *R* of relocation in their three-*R* strategy (relocation, reconciliation and redistribution), it seemed like a very risky and radical move. Little did they realize that in a couple of short decades, the dangerous ghettos into which they urged urban workers to move would become the high-rent districts of loft apartments, condos, avant-garde art studios and gourmet eateries. Never could they have imagined that relocating for ministry purposes into a community of need and buying and renovating a home would be the very spark that would ignite the fires of gentrification—a movement that is now displacing the poor at an alarming rate from those very neighborhoods. The urban landscape is indeed changing, and with that change, our ministry strategies must change if we are to remain effective agents of both compassion and justice.

Urban ministries, then, are at a crossroad. Those committed to long-term relationships with the poor are discovering that their low-income neighbors are slowly but steadily disappearing from their neighborhoods. The affordable rental houses and apartments that have been homes for the poor for generations are being sold and renovated, and rents are skyrocketing. In an attempt to maintain relationships with their members (most often the youth in their programs), urban ministries are purchasing vans to shuttle participants back to their centers. But this strategy is proving to be stop-gap at best. The cost of vans, insurance, gas and driving time eventually reaches the point of diminishing returns, and ministries face the hard reality that their centers will no longer hold. They face a T in the road.

One option for these churches is to change their facility-centered programs and become migrant ministries that follow the streams of poor who are migrating out to the less expensive, class-B apartment complexes in the inner-ring suburbs. There they can establish satellite ministry centers that will be mobile and flexible enough to shift with the demographic tides. In these cases, though, the church center in the inner city may lose much of its strategic value and may need to be adapted for other uses that better fit the changing community there. But the benefit of this option is that it affords the opportunity to keep relationships intact over time.

Another direction is community development, an option that enables low-income residents to remain in the neighborhood and participate in the benefits of a reviving community. This requires an even larger shift in ministry strategy. It involves real estate development—an area in which few urban ministries have had experience. In order to retain affordable housing in a gentrifying community, land and/or buildings must be purchased before their value appreciates. This calls for new sources of funds and new ways of financing. A professional revitalization plan must be designed that demonstrates the economic feasibility of mixed-income development—a requirement if a ministry is to attract the substantial loans and grants required to implement the vision. Such a community development strategy obviously calls for a range of talents (architecture, engineering, construction, financing, property management, to name a few) not commonly found among urban ministries. The good news, of course, is that these talents are abundant in the pews of the more affluent churches. The challenge is to connect these marketplace gifts to a Kingdom vision in the city. New partnerships must be formed, new organizational structures must be created, new funding sources must be identified—these are the essential new technologies of compassion that are needed to do justice in the changing urban world.

Gentrification is a new national norm. The returning wave of professional classes (and their resources) builds with steady momentum while the less affluent are pushed to the periphery. Though gentrification is necessary for the rebuilding of our cities, the injustice involved in the process is not. The people of faith who know the heart of God and believe in the central importance of loving one's neighbor have the capacity to bring about gentrification with justice. We can influence public policies that ensure mixed-income (inclusionary) zoning; we can forge partnerships with visionary real estate developers to create affordable housing; we can create investment funds to acquire and manage apartments. Such models already exist, in fact, and the current experience base is now sufficient enough to begin studying to find out which are the best practices.

The scope of this book permits neither a detailed exploration of gentrification nor a description of the innovative programs that urban ministries are attempting as they work for justice in their changing communities. Rather, it is the intent of this writing to describe how human development (as opposed to non-reciprocal services and programs) can enhance the life of a community for all its residents, both rich and poor. Old paradigms of one-way giving, though compassionate and well-meaning, must be revisited just as surely as must the three *R*s of Christian Community Development. This book is an attempt at a candid reexamination of our common methods of charity. Hopefully it will be useful in stimulating new technologies of compassion for the age of gentrification.

INTRODUCTION

This book grew out of a discussion the author and a concerned philanthropist had over the surprising "NIMBY" (not in my back yard) response that urban neighborhoods often voice when a ministry moves in. It would seem, from the outside at least, that a blighted community would be eager to receive any help it could to address its overwhelming needs. Not so. If there is any sense of community spirit still burning, any hope that the neighborhood can be restored to health, active residents will instead be busy organizing crime watches, pursuing businesses that they want to return, supporting efforts to improve the local schools, and a host of other initiatives that they hope will stimulate new life. The community will oppose—sometimes forcefully—any activity that it perceives to be a detriment to community resurgence.

It often comes as a shock to ministry-minded people that the community negatively views good programs (like churches or drug treatment centers). Pastors, for example, cannot fathom why a neighborhood would oppose church expansion, which from their point of view only serves to strengthen the moral fiber and spiritual vitality of a community. The same is often true of human service agencies like halfway houses and supported-living facilities.

Having been a resident of an urban neighborhood for nearly three decades as well as having started a number of programs (including a church, subsidized housing, and social service centers) in my community, I have had the opportunity to view this issue from both sides. I have had stand-offs with angry homeowners over building affordable housing next door to them. I also have been at odds with churches that wanted to expand their facilities and parking capacity at the expense of residential land. I have rallied residents to turn out at zoning hearings at city hall in support of special-use permits required to license a group home for adolescent offenders. I have also lobbied city counsel members to block the location of yet another supported-living facility for mentally challenged persons in our neighborhood.

Somewhere in the tension between service-providing institutions and the neighborhoods that are impacted by them, there is a reasonable common ground, or at least a place to work out compromises. This book is an attempt to expose some of the thorny issues that communities and service providers grapple over and to offer some practical suggestions for their amicable resolution. I must confess my bias, however. *I am a community developer first and a social service provider second. Any service that in any way compromises the strengthening of community fabric, I will side against—including the Church.*

Having said that, I also recognize that not all community-building activities or activists embrace justice as one of their priorities. Some gentrifiers would feel fine about displacing all of the poor from their neighborhood. Some historic purists would impose housing codes so restrictive that only middle-income homeowners could afford to keep up. Some educated parents would think nothing of creating a community charter school that would effectively segregate out lower-income children. Not all community development serves the whole community equally well. And so there remains a tension between self-interest and community interest.

It seems to me that an important role of the Kingdom-minded person is to walk in the midst of those tensions, advocating the well-being of the community and the interests of the most vulnerable, both at the same time. Ours is a vision of not only a thriving community, but of a just one as well.

PART I

WHAT'S WRONG WITH THIS PICTURE?

Something doesn't seem right. We can't lay our finger on it, but it just doesn't feel right. Our calling to minister to the needs of the poor is unquestionable. Scripture is abundantly clear about this mandate. And our hearts feel full when we spend ourselves on behalf of the oppressed. This is, indeed, very pleasing to God. But something deep inside troubles us. We wonder if the money we dropped into the Styrofoam cup of a homeless man actually helps him, or if it merely supports his addiction. When we see the same families show up week after week at our church food pantry, we can't help questioning (though very privately) whether we are helping them get on their feet or whether we are fostering their dependency. We attempt to do justice and love mercy, only to have our neighbors turn on us and oppose our good works.

Rightly serving those in need is no simple matter. And attempting to restore broken communities is even more complicated. It raises matters we never anticipated when we first responded from the heart to get involved in the city.

In this section, we will explore some of these disquieting issues. In the form of vignettes of personal experiences, we will probe some of the underlying dilemmas that caring people encounter as we attempt to faithfully carry out the teachings of Scripture to become personally involved with "the least of these" (Matt. 5:19).

CHAPTER 1

WHAT DOES JESUS SAY?

Some time ago, I was invited to address the student body of a Bible college well known for its strong commitment to the authority of Scripture. It was "urban emphasis" week, and I was asked to be the keynote speaker to kick off the event. The most enjoyable part of my time on campus was interacting in the classroom with eager students who voiced many insightful questions about ministry in the city.

During a lively discussion with a group of upperclassmen, I posed the question, "What is the number-one mandate for the followers of Christ?"

"Evangelize!" came the immediate and emphatic response.

I pushed them a little harder: "But what did Christ *say* was top priority?"

There was a slight pause. "Make disciples," they responded, offering a slight modification to their initial answer.

"I know that evangelizing and making disciples is important," I agreed, "but what did Christ *actually say* was that most important mandate for His followers?"

After a moment or two of puzzled silence, a student in the back of the classroom ventured a hesitant response: "You mean 'Thou shalt love the Lord thy God with all thine heart, mind, soul and strength and thy neighbor as thyself'?"

"Is this what He said was number one?" I continued to push. There were head-nods and another student added, "On this hang all the law and the prophets." These young people had their Scripture down well.

"I agree with you," I concurred. "That's how I read it, too. Our Lord called it the greatest command, didn't He?" There seemed to be consensus. "Given that Scripture declares this to be our number-one mandate, then what courses do you have here on neighboring? I know you have an entire department of evangelism. Who teaches Neighboring 101?"

There was an uncomfortable silence as the implications of my question began to sink in. "We don't have any courses on neighboring," they reluctantly admitted.

"Not a single course?" I questioned again. Stone silence. "The greatest command of Scripture and you don't have *even one* course on it? Then this Bible College is just not biblical enough," I declared.

"Do you believe in a literal heaven and a literal hell?" one sharp young theology student retorted. I knew the rationale behind his question. If you believe that either eternal bliss or eternal damnation awaits every person after death, then the most loving act is to present the truth of the gospel to as many people as possible and thus save them from everlasting destruction.

It's a compelling argument. The problem, of course, is that it leads toward viewing others as souls instead of people. And when we opt for rescuing souls over loving neighbors, compassionate acts can soon degenerate into evangelism techniques; pressing human needs depreciate in importance, and the spirit becomes the only thing worth caring about. Thus, the powerful leaven of unconditional, sacrificial love is diminished in society and the wounded are left lying beside the road. When we skip over the Great Commandment on the way to fulfilling the Great Commission, we do great harm to the authenticity of the faith.

"I can see you have your theology buttoned down well," I conceded. "But I think the more important question is, 'What did *Christ* say we should be about?'" Silence again.

So fundamental to the life of faith are these twin teachings of loving God and loving neighbor that they are given top priority in God's original handwritten instructions for daily living. Christ later underscored their central importance by declaring that the entire law is contained in these two inseparable commands. A Christian training institute (or church, for that matter) that steps over these basics on the way to "deeper" theological pursuits can hardly be considered biblically faithful. (I have not been invited back to the school to speak.)

CHAPTER 2

WHAT ABOUT ROOT CAUSES?

"Who sinned here?" the disciples asked Jesus as they approached a blind man sitting, cup in hand, on a narrow Jerusalem street. A curbside beggar who had been blind from the moment he emerged from his mother's womb was calling out to them for alms. Unlike other beggars who had lost their capacity to earn a living due to some sickness or unfortunate accident, this man had been born stone blind.

A tragedy like this doesn't just *happen*—it is *caused*. And obviously his blindness could not be his own fault. What hidden sin had been committed to bring this awful curse upon a baby? Perhaps it was his parents' wrongdoing, maybe venereal disease or some sort of prenatal abuse.

"Why did it happen, Jesus? Who is really to blame here?" It was an important issue that the disciples raised. If they could get to the root cause, then perhaps they could discover the key to preventing tragedies like this in the future. At the very least, they could pin down the guilty culprit and identify this deformity for what it really was—God's judgment upon sin.

"Who sinned here?" we ask, as a pale, stringy-haired teenage girl brings her premature infant, quivering from fetal alcohol syndrome, into the health clinic. How did things go so very wrong so early in these young lives to cause such irreparable harm? Is it the fault of this young mother, too weak-willed to put the needs of her unborn baby above her own self-indulgence? Or should we blame her addicted, live-in lover who got her hooked on drugs and alcohol in the first place? Or maybe it's society's fault, our materialistic culture too consumed with self-interest to notice the swelling epidemic of social pathology that ravages the poor. And where is the Church amidst all this suffering? This issue of cause (or more precisely, blame) is large in *our* minds, too, Jesus.

But Jesus does not answer the disciples' question in the way they expect. Bypassing the issue of blame altogether, He seizes an opportune moment to reveal a secret of the Kingdom. Looking directly into the beggar's filmy eyes that have never gazed upon a Palestinian sunrise, He says, "This has happened so that the power of God may be seen at work in him."

What a strange and unexpected twist! Blindness is an opportunity for new sight! The atmosphere tensed with excitement as the Teacher bent down, mixed a salve of available elements of the earth, smoothed it over the man's eyes, and gave him easy-to-follow instructions to wash it off in the nearby pool.

The curious crowd that had collected to observe this unusual spectacle jostled along behind the blind man as he tapped his way to the pool and stooped to cup handfuls of water onto his face. In an instant, sunlight streamed into his darkened eyes. And into his soul flooded the light of spiritual dawn. The man who was born blind threw aside his cane and cup and ran with wide-eyed amazement up and down the streets of the city, reveling in a panorama he had only vaguely imagined. It was a sight to behold!

"For judgment I have come into this world, so that the blind will see and those who see will become blind," Jesus soberly informed His disciples after the crowd had gone. It was one of those troubling, riddle-type remarks that only those closest to Him would decipher. Yes, He would pronounce judgment, this He admitted, but not of the blaming sort. His indictments would come in the form of sight-loss for the "enlightened ones" who are more concerned with affixing blame than with extending mercy.

Those who spend their time searching for someone to accuse rather than looking expectantly for divine opportunity, even though they have 20/20 eyesight, will show themselves to be blind leaders of the blind. As Helen Keller described it, "The greatest handicap is to have sight and no vision."

"But certainly finding root causes can be important, can't it, Teacher?" we feel compelled to inquire. Medical science has enabled us to prevent untold suffering and save countless lives. We have nearly eradicated infant blindness, and we know how to contain communicable diseases. How can this knowledge be anything but good?

The Master answers by His example, His touch, His personal attentiveness. He shows us that cure without care is not the Kingdom way. Knowledge and even self-sacrifice, unless accompanied by love, are of little worth in His economy. He invites us to slip in a little closer so that we can see for ourselves that the darkness of sightless eyes is not as intense as the despair of the soul of one who is discarded. In coming close we begin to see that the withdrawal pains of an addicted mother are no more excruciating than the torment of feeling less than worthless. And if we take the risk of personally touching and being touched by a suffering person, the miracle of sight can break into *our own* darkness. When the clarity of compassion illuminates our vision, we can visualize healing that goes far deeper than physical cure. Through eyes of faith we recognize that this could be an opportunity for tragedy to be transformed into celebration so that the power of God may be seen at work in him and in her.

And even more amazing, when we stoop to personally touch one of these "undesirables" with hands-on care, we are touching the very heart of God: "I tell you the truth, whatever you did for one of the least of these brothers [and sisters] of mine, you did for me" (Matt. 25:40, *NIV*).

CHAPTER 3

SERVING AND CONTROLLING

She looked to me to be in her late 50s, gray hair bushing out beneath her knit cap. She grasped a large shopping-bag-type purse with one hand and pounded persistently on the church door with the other. We could see her through the hazy Plexiglas window as the pastor and I walked down the hall, the lively discussion of our early morning meeting on homelessness still fresh on our minds.

"The clothes closet opens at 10. You can come back and get some clothes then," the pastor informed her, with as much sensitivity as any busy urban leader who is running late for his next meeting. "No, no!" she interrupted before the sentence had barely escaped his lips, her countenance visibly fallen. "I'm here to help sort clothes." But the damage was done. The spirit that had moved this little lady to get up early in the morning to help clothe others had been wounded. A simple error. Understandable. Unwittingly made. Irreversible.

"It is more blessed to give than to receive" (Acts 20:35), our Lord told His followers. The blessedness of rising early to serve others in need had been marred by identifying the little lady as a recipient of charity rather than a giver. Her face reflected the hurt that the loss of self-esteem can inflict.

Receiving, I am beginning to realize, is a humbling thing. It implies neediness. It categorizes one as being "worse off" than the giver. Perhaps it is for this reason that we tend to reserve for ourselves the "more blessed" position.

One thing that has been troubling me about our diverse urban congregation is the lack of authentic reconciliation between the "have-a-lots" and "have-a-littles." The little lady in the knit cap may be showing us where part of our difficulty lies. I came to the city to serve those in need. I have been given resources and abilities to clothe the ill-clad, feed the hungry, shelter the homeless—good works that our Lord requires of us. There is blessedness in this kind of giving, to be sure. But there is also power in it—which can be dangerous. Giving allows me to retain control. Retaining the helping position protects me from the humiliation of appearing to need help. And, even more sobering, I condemn those whom I would help to the permanent, prideless role of recipient.

When my motivation is to change people, I inadvertently communicate: Something is wrong with you, but (quite subtly) I am okay. If our relationship is defined as healer/patient, then I must remain well and they must remain sick in order for our interaction to continue. Since one does not go to the doctor when he is well, curing, then, cannot long serve as the basis for any relationship that is life-enhancing for both participants. Little wonder that we, who have come to the city to "save" the poor, find it difficult to enter into true community with those we deem needy.

Scripture describes a Kingdom comprised of diverse people with all manner of gifts and talents. Each citizen of this heaven-based Kingdom has been given an important work to do. Those with the highest standing in heaven are the people who, in our earthly value system, are considered least important.

It is disquieting to realize how little value I attribute to "the least of these," the ones deemed by our Lord to be "great in the Kingdom" (Matt. 5:19, *NIV*). I have viewed them as weak ones waiting to be rescued, not bearers of divine treasures. The dominance of my giving overshadows and stifles the rich endowments that the Creator has invested in those I have considered destitute. I selectively ignore that the moneyed, empowered, learned ones will enter this Kingdom with enormous difficulty.

One who would be a leader, I am cautioned, has a greater weight of responsibility to honor the despised, share his earthly possessions, model interdependency and encourage the use of gifts concealed in the unlikeliest among us. To the leader, then, the gift of humility is offered—the gift is the salvation of the proud, which comes with great difficulty from learning to receive from those who are the least on Earth, yet greatest in the Kingdom.

CHAPTER 4

CLOTHES CLOSETS
AND COMPASSION

While volunteering on a remodeling project in our inner city church, I came across a yellowed paper sign taped to the wall of an old storage room. "Clothes Closet," it was entitled. I glanced at it casually before snatching it down. A closer look revealed it to be more than an old sign—it was an important historical document. Its lined-out, crayoned-in revisions and parenthesized explanations told a fascinating story of the evolution of a ministry. Between its lines one could read of a classic struggle between Christians in charge and people in need. I gently peeled the document from its place to preserve it for further study.

Look carefully at the sign and you can decipher unwritten content between the lines. The minimum 10-cent charge is the first attempt to control the greed of recipients who were abusing the church's generosity. The scratched-out 10 to 15 garment price rates reveal the obvious failure to adequately limit the abuse. Then, there's the sentiment that goes something like, okay, five articles total, that's it! And the qualification: Unless a receiver gets a note signed by one of the pastors, NO CREDIT! No money, no admission—nice and clear. Keeping track of credit accounts is too complicated and time-consuming and collecting unpaid debts is just too troublesome. Then it becomes: no free clothes without a special *written* dispensation from one of the preachers. This rule is designed to curb the informal end-runs around the system. Only an ordained minister can authorize exceptions to the rules. All sales and recipients will be reported to the Christian Council. This documentation is designed to cut off

No Smoking

GEORGIA AVENUE PRESBYTERIAN CHURCH
645 GRANT STREET
ATLANTA, GEORGIA

CLOTHES CLOSET
Beginning January 1, 1962

THERE WILL BE A MINIMUM CHARGE OF 10¢ FOR EACH USE OF
THE CLOTHES CLOSET!

          Clothes Closet Pay Scale
     Up to 5 articles for 10¢.   :

     Up to 10 articles for 20¢.   : - NO CREDIT

     Up to 15 articles for 30¢.   :

****

     No one may use the clothes closet without charge
     unless they have first done these three things:
     1. Talked with Rev. Hicks or Rev. Rosenberger.
     2. Get a signed note from one of these pastors.
     3. Present the note to the clothes closet operator

     No one may take more than 5 articles without doing
     these three things first:
     1. Talk with Rev. Hicks or Rev Rosenberger.
     2. Get a signed note from one of them verifying your
        need to take more than 15 garments.
     3. Present the note to the clothes closet operator.

* A pair of anything which comes in pairs will count as one
article.

     ****

     A regular report of services rendered by this church is
made to the Welfare Division of the Christian Council of
Metropolitan Atlanta.

          (The words "no one" shall be taken to mean
          either individuals or families.)

those who are making the rounds to churches all over the city. The interpretation of the meaning "no one" requires clarification. The five-garment limit is for one family, not five articles for every family member. No smoking. Of course.

Can you envision the challenging, the tightening of rules, the manipulative ploys, the counter-moves that transpired between good church folk and those they were trying to help? Like temple police, they enacted their one-sided legislation and diligently guarded the resources of the Kingdom as if they were their own.

Somewhere in the process of ministering, the poor became their adversaries.

Anyone who has been given the unfortunate task of dispensing free (or nearly free) commodities will soon have familiar war stories to tell. Something seems to go wrong when one with valued resources attempts to distribute them to others in need. The transactions, no matter how compassionate, seem to go sour in the gut of both giver and recipient. A subtle, unintentional message slips through: "You have nothing of worth that I desire in return." The giver remains protected by his one-up status while the recipient is exposed and vulnerable. Little wonder that negative attitudes surface. It becomes hard to be a cheerful giver—and even harder to be a cheerful recipient.

Ancient Hebrew wisdom describes four levels of charity. The highest level is to provide a job for one in need without his knowledge that you provided it. The next, lower level is to provide work that the needy one knows you provided. The third level is to give an anonymous gift to meet an immediate need. The lowest level of charity, to be avoided if at all possible, is to give a poor person a gift with his full knowledge that you are the donor.

Perhaps the deepest poverty of all is to have nothing of value to offer in exchange. Charity that fosters such poverty must be challenged. We know from 40 years of failed social policy that welfare depletes self-esteem while honorable work produces dignity. We know that reciprocity builds mutual respect while one-way giving brews contempt. Yet we continue to run clothes closets and free food pantries and give-away benevolence accounts and wonder why the joy is missing.

Perhaps it is our time and place in history to re-implement the wisdom of the ages and to fashion contemporary models of thoughtful compassion. Our donated clothes could create thrift store and job training. Our benevolence dollars could develop mini-economies within the economy—daycare, janitorial, fix-the-widow's-roof services that would employ the jobless in esteem-building work. "Your work is your calling," declared the reformer, Luther. Does not the role of the Church in our day include the enabling of the poor to find their calling?

CHAPTER 5

COMMUNITY-FRIENDLY CHURCH

Through the trees in my backyard, I can see the steeple of the Lighthouse Tabernacle Holiness Church, Inc. It's a charming church with white columns and a neatly manicured landscape. For as long as neighborhood residents can remember, it has maintained a quiet presence on the street. Its Sunday morning worshipers fit easily into the church parking lot, and the sounds of music and preaching are well contained within the air-conditioned sanctuary. It can genuinely be said of the Lighthouse Tabernacle Holiness Church, Inc. that it does no harm to our community.

That is not to say that the church is community-friendly, however. It is just not community-unfriendly. Some neighbors even remember that a few years back, church members went door-to-door inviting community children to enroll in their summer vacation Bible school. But they haven't done that for some time now. Like most of the churches in our neighborhood, Lighthouse Tabernacle Holiness Church, Inc. is a commuter church and neither pastor nor parishioners live in the area. Because they drive in from other places, they have little vested interest in the neighborhood—except, of course, interest in their building, which they maintain beautifully.

In 1934 (the date on its cornerstone), the church was a vital part of the life of the neighborhood. It served as a moral compass and spiritual strand in the fabric of the community. The pastor lived in a parsonage next door and his children attended the neighborhood schools. His voice carried authority when he attended PTA meetings because he spoke not only for his own children but also for those of his congregation.

Tithes and offerings stayed largely in the community, paying for salaries, youth programs, benevolence for those in need and, of course, the building. When the church bought the adjacent lot to build an educational wing, the neighborhood was supportive. What was good for the church, they knew, was good for the community. That's when the church was *of* the community.

Over time, however, members moved to the suburbs and eventually the church was sold to another group. The new pastor owned a home in another part of the city and had no need for the parsonage. The new congregation was friendly enough, but their busy lives were invested elsewhere. Their community outreach efforts were well-intentioned but lacked consistency. And they gave the subtle impression that they viewed neighborhood folk as "the lost," which seemed not a very community-friendly theology. Though the church building continued to be attractively maintained, the church was no longer of the community.

Expressways and multiple-car families have changed everything—especially the Church—over the past 50 years. From an institution rooted in the soil of community, the Church has become a spiritual health club for commuters. Pastors now measure their success by the number of ZIP codes from which they draw their membership. Accessibility and parking have become two of the church's greatest challenges. Church growth consultants advise locating on a visible site along an expressway, near an exit for easy access. In a strange twist of history, church growth has fallen subject to the same impact studies required of amphitheatres and shopping centers.

As it has conformed to the commuter age, the Church must now be scrutinized for its disruptiveness to neighborhoods. For example, a watershed decision took place several years ago in Atlanta when the largest, most powerful church in my denomination applied to the city for a permit to build yet another addition to its already huge facility. To everyone's disbelief, they were turned down flat—something that had not happened before to a church in that area. The premise had always been, what's good for the church is good for the community. But not this time. Neighbors showed up en masse at public hearings to protest. Enough jammed streets. Enough blocked driveways. Enough police directing traffic on their residential streets. And the city listened. The substantial political and legal muscle that the church was able to summon was unable to reverse the city council's vote.

From that landmark decision onward, churches in Atlanta have had great difficulty obtaining building permits because they have been without strong support from the "impacted" community. Even a large youth center proposed by the mega World Changers church, arguably a needed resource for the youth on the south side, was recently turned down by the city because of congestion issues.

Many religious leaders are convinced that this resistance to church growth is a manifestation of demonic opposition to the work of God's kingdom. I have a different opinion. Rather than demonic, I believe it is prophetic. This new phenomenon of community resistance to churches is not so much the influence of "principalities and powers" (Eph. 3:10, *KJV*) subverting the work of God as it is the cry of a people whose churches are no longer part of the life of their communities. It is more a plea than a protest, I believe, that arises out of the soul of a society that has lost a fundamental social mooring—community.

When our culture traded front-porch neighborhood life for private backyard patios, when we succumbed to the seduction of individualism and lost touch with our next-door neighbors, a void was created in the spirit of our people that chat rooms cannot fill. The commuting church, with its scattered members buzzing in and out of the neighborhood, is one more troubling reminder of what we have lost. A community-starved society, by its protests, is calling the Church back to its historic mandate: to be the exemplar within the community of both love of God and love of neighbor.

PART II

IS IT TIME TO CONSIDER A CHANGE?

Doing for others what they can do for themselves is charity at its worst. New technologies of charity must be developed to bring the dignity of reciprocity into the practice. We must come to deeply believe that every person, no matter how destitute or broken, has something of worth to bring to the table. And although the alternatives to one-way charity may be complex to create, this underlying belief in the necessity for every human to pull his full capacity will guide us toward healthy mutuality with those we would assist.

What is true for individuals is also true for communities. Loading a depressed neighborhood with human services, while at first pass may seem curative, may in fact be the very approach that keeps a community from rebounding. Doing for a community what it could do for itself is as damaging to community life as it is to an individual.

Further, the scale often required by serving institutions to operate cost-effectively may well require the importing of need from other communities. The last thing a struggling neighborhood needs is to have even more addicted, homeless, mentally ill or jobless people flooding into its streets. New technologies of compassion require us to rethink our economies of scale in order that our service becomes community-friendly.

In the following section we will delve more deeply into the underlying dynamics of serving and suggest some possible alternatives to the ways we have traditionally attempted to care for the poor.

CHAPTER 6

HELPING JOHN

"There's something I'd like your opinion on." John stared intently at me over the steam of two freshly brewed cups of coffee. He wasted no time on playful banter, which was unlike his typical way of greeting me when we get together for our monthly breakfasts at the OK Cafe. He had just come from an early morning men's Bible study and was obviously perplexed by something.

"What am I supposed to do with all these people who want something from me?" John had money and a lot of people knew it. Daily—sometimes several times a day—he got letters and calls from people imploring him for help with some cause or personal need. He could handle the letters and the phone calls, he said. It was the pleading eyes of a person in some desperate financial crisis that got to him. A struggling father whose family was about to be put out on the street if he couldn't come up with immediate rent money; a pleading young woman at a gas station who needed $27.15 to get her car out of repair so that she could get home to Alabama; a hungry homeless man outside of church asking for a dollar for a bite to eat. "What is a Christian supposed to do with these kinds of requests?" he asked.

"I know, I know," he preempted my response. "Get involved—take the homeless man to McDonald's." He was obviously hoping for a different answer from me, something more insightful. After all, I have spent most of my adult life serving among the poor in the inner city. I should know about these things. Of all people, I should know how to deal responsibly with people in need.

Those who come away empty-handed from their encoun-
ters with John might well judge him to be just another penny-
pinching businessman. They would be wrong. Those who know
John as well as I do would know that in fact he is quite the opposite. John gives generously of his considerable means, especially
to those ministries and causes that he deeply believes in. But he
has little patience with people who shirk their own personal
responsibilities. And another thing that perturbs him is when
he discovers that a contribution that was solicited for one purpose has been spent on another. That's one reason he is so thor-
ough in his due diligence before he writes a check. He will research
how much a 501(c)3 organization spends on marketing and
overhead. He even requests a printout of his church's annual
financial statement.

But how can he know that a gift to a homeless person will
go for food and not for booze? And even if he does take a half
hour out of his hectic day to sit down over a Big Mac with a
street person, how can he know that he is not simply enabling
the man to continue an irresponsible lifestyle?

Several Scriptures were fresh on John's mind, obviously a
carry-over from the morning's Bible study. Feeding the hungry,
clothing the naked, giving your second coat, lending to those
who can't repay . . . and the final convicting blow—"inasmuch
as you did it to one of the least of these, my bretheren, you did
it to Me" (Matt. 25:40) and the damning converse about not
doing so. Had John been turning away Christ when he refused
to give to those so obviously in desperate need? The thought
haunted him.

I wanted to be wise. And profound. I wished that I had gone
to seminary and could explain the meaning of the original texts.
But, in fact, all I had to go on were 30 years of pragmatic trial
and error, a modicum of common sense, and intuition jaded
just a bit by hearing too many deceptions and half truths. And,

oh yes, a calling to the poor that had been the orienting compass needle in my life.

Three decades of serving in the city should have fine-tuned my compassion skills, but, as I confessed to John, I feel as furious as he does when I learn that the young woman at the gas station has used that same $27.15 story on scores of suckers at dozens of gas stations around town. But could it be that our reluctance to give to the stranger on the street is much more than a reaction conditioned by cons we have fallen prey to? Could our hesitance be a righteous response from our spirit cautioning us that irresponsible giving is detrimental both to the recipient and the giver?

There is one thing that both John and I readily agree upon: Deep satisfaction registers within us when we give of ourselves to meet a legitimate human need—like stopping to help at the scene of an accident or comforting a lost child who is frantically searching for her mother in a mall. When the need is real and the situation critical, we will gladly sacrifice our time, resources and even personal safety to rescue someone from trouble. Our desire to help others is the imprint of our Creator on our lives.

There is also, however, something quite opposite and equally poignant that reacts in our spirits when we encounter a grave injustice. Like the kind-talking confidence man who defrauds an aging widow out of her life savings or the executive who embezzles from his workers their hard-earned retirement funds—our outrage at such despicable behavior also reflects the image of our Creator.

Why, then, does John feel so guilty walking past the panhandler with the "Homeless, please help, God bless you" sign when there is virtually no way to determine where a gift will go? Is it really a charitable act to support the questionable (and likely self-destructive) habits of a stranger when John would refuse to do the same for his own son?

We raise our children to become self-sufficient, responsible adults. We push them to develop their potential. We try our best to keep them away from drugs and bad influences that would ensnare them. But if our best efforts fail, if tragically, offspring choose a path toward self-destruction, tough love will eventually necessitate our cutting off support.

Our anguish intensifies when their "friends" deepen the entrapment by sharing their beds and needles. Is there really any way for John to know that his $27.15 will not add to the torment of some grieving parents as well as deepen the dependency of their prodigal daughter?

So why the guilt? Is it false guilt arising out of the "oughts" and "shoulds" that we have picked up from parents and preachers?

John and I broke into laughter recalling the tactics of a couple of homeless guys who occasionally wait outside our church on Sunday morning. Refuse their appeal and their pitiful "help me" expressions quickly turn to "and you call yourself a Christian" sneers. They certainly know their audience. We couldn't decide which emotion was stronger—guilt from being uncharitable or anger at their manipulation.

These homeless entrepreneurs have learned what relief agencies have known for a long time—pity is a powerful motivator. If you can properly portray a picture of desperation, whether a starving child or a disheveled beggar, the human heart instinctively responds. The more seasoned solicitors have refined their presentations to draw the prospective donor into the plight with just the right mix of misery and hope. Too much anguish and the viewer is grossed out; too much hope and he gets away guilt-free.

At least the guys outside our church get the satisfaction of turning the knife in a lost prospect, we chuckled. The comic relief felt good. That we could so nonchalantly pass by the hungry did not. We were suddenly back to John's original question.

No, we should not give irresponsibly. Buying drugs or alcohol for an addicted person is not responsible. Neither is accepting a warm feeling in exchange for dropping money into a cup. Yet, what about those with mental illness who have fallen through the cracks? And the abused mother who has fled for safety with her children and landed in a shelter?

For some, hot soup and clean clothes and a dollar in the cup are life-preserving sources. Admittedly, this sort of one-way charity is demeaning for the recipient, but then, desperation is a prideless place to be. But is there any way we can decipher whether the story we are hearing is true or fabricated?

There is another means of assisting, of course, that hardly requires any verification. Work. If you hire a person to do legitimate work for reasonable pay, the exchange is honorable and dignifying regardless of how the person chooses to spend the money. But really, how realistic is it for John to take off work to create a job and spend the day supervising a homeless man? Better to support a program that is in this business—a little thing I call due diligence.

Due diligence. That's the best answer I could come up with. Due diligence and the prompting of the Spirit. Once on an infrequent occasion, you may have an inner nudging that tells you to stop immediately and help a person. You don't know why, but there's just a strong impression that you should offer money or food or a ride. There's no rational explanation. This may well be the Divine Spirit at work in ways we will not understand until the curtain of eternity is pulled back. There are no assurances, but it's worth the risk. Other than this, due diligence is my answer. If you don't have time to invest in forging a trusting relationship, give your money to a ministry that does.

John thought that my answer might be a little self-serving. Maybe he was right.

CHAPTER 7

BETTERMENT TO DEVELOPMENT

When a community has suffered from years of neglect, when rental properties have deteriorated and trash has piled up on vacant lots, when the city no longer replaces shot-out streetlights or fixes potholes on the road, almost any positive activity is welcomed.

Even welcome are the naïve youth from suburban churches who arrive on Saturday mornings to eagerly fill dumpsters with old tires and collect mounds of debris in garbage bags. Seniors who watch from behind dead-bolted doors, dismayed that their neighborhood has lost the sense of pride it once had, are nevertheless pleased that something—anything—positive is taking place on their streets.

Help is badly needed when conditions in a community have reached such a low ebb. Latchkey kids need activities that provide alternatives to the destructive influences of the street. They need after-school programs to bolster inadequate public education and offer safe environments while their mothers are still at work. But the under-funded Boys' and Girls' Clubs in tired old facilities, though important, are insufficient. And what about the homebound seniors who need someone to fix their leaking roofs and repair their rotting porches? New blood is badly needed—fresh volunteers, new initiatives, new vision and passion.

In declining urban communities there is no shortage of need. And for those looking for real needs to address, this is the ideal place to focus. Clothes closets, food pantries, tutoring, weekend service projects, summer camps, recreation programs—all these and a host of other hands-on activities can make a significant difference in the lives of kids and seniors, and can help ease the load for working moms.

We can describe this kind of personal involvement as "betterment" activities. Betterment activities offer relief from difficult situations and improve the existing conditions. Sometimes a hardy soul within the neighborhood will attempt such efforts, but most often, programs are initiated by and dependent upon the good will of outsiders. People of compassion—often visionary, mission-minded people, even "called" people—who are motivated to minister to the poor bring much needed programs, resources and care to a depleted neighborhood. Yet, as important as these services may be (essential, some would say), *serving* people is distinctly different from *developing* people.

Betterment *does for* others; development enables others to *do for themselves*. Betterment improves conditions; development strengthens capacity. Betterment gives a man a fish; development teaches a man how to fish.

Most of the programs we create to help people in need begin as betterment projects. This is understandable. When our hearts are touched as we encounter a pressing human need and when we realize that we have the capacity (yes, even the responsibility) to meet that need, we quite naturally seek ways to address that need in the most direct and immediate means at our disposal. A homeless man is hungry, so we offer him food. A bright child is failing in school, so we help her with her homework. An aging widow's heat has been cut off, so we pay her gas bill. These are personal acts of compassion that address an immediate, correctable need. Of course this is where we begin—with a felt need.

It follows, then, that if we are moved to address the needs of more hungry people or educationally disadvantaged children or neglected seniors, we will begin to explore methods that are more efficient than a one-on-one approach. We establish food pantries, tutoring classes and adopt-a-grandparent programs that touch many more people in need. We may even envision strategies to eliminate hunger entirely from a community, to raise the standard of education for all area students or to see that every homebound elder has a caring volunteer. This is the stuff of vision. This is the milieu in which prototype ministry models are born.

But efficiency is not the same as effectiveness. A superbly run food pantry, complete with balanced menu, dependable supply sources and computer accountability, still does little to develop recipients' capacities to become self-sufficient. On the contrary, free food distribution does more to create dependency than encourage healthy independency. The same is true of clothes closets and community clean-ups. The best-run betterment programs, though admirable examples of well-run systems, do little to strengthen the community's capacity to address its own needs. They may even work at cross-purposes with community development.

I experienced firsthand the unintended consequences of a betterment program the year I moved into the city. The need in the community for decent, affordable clothing was immediately obvious—a need that could be easily addressed through the network of affluent churches that supported our ministry. The vacant neighborhood church that we reopened had a large, unused storage room that seemed the perfect place for a community clothes closet. (Chapter four describes the old congregation's earlier attempts to serve the community through their clothes closet.) In no time, we had a brightly painted, well-organized, well-stocked, free "clothing outlet" open for business.

But as soon as the first customers came through the door, the spirit of charity that smiling volunteers exuded faded rapidly. A hoarding instinct (the same kind of I-gotta-get-mine impulse that seizes looting crowds) took over our customers as they grabbed and growled and stuffed as many clothes into as many trash bags as they could carry. It was pure bedlam.

Rules had to be hastily enacted. (We could have taken lessons from the tattered and yellowed "rules" sign from the prior clothes closet that we found taped to the wall.) But this was a new day and we would face these challenges with fresh vigor! Three garments per visit. One visit per week. This provided a modicum of order; it was also like saying, "Let the games begin."

Customers probed to find the limits and loopholes of these rapidly conceived regulations. Could they get three articles of clothing for each of their children who were in school? Could they get three garments for their sick uncle who couldn't make it to the church? An adversarial relationship soon developed between those in charge and those in need. In no time at all, our volunteers were behaving like temple police guarding the resources of the Kingdom against the very people we had intended to serve.

"There's a simple solution to that problem," we were informed by a Methodist men's group from one of our supporting Atlanta churches. "It's called 'the market.'" If we put a fair rate of exchange on a desired commodity, they counseled, it would eliminate all the hoarding behavior.

Sell the clothes; don't give them away. People will then buy only what they can afford. And if they have no clothing money, they can work in the store and earn what they need. This would produce cash flow, the men said, that would enable us to hire unemployed residents, train them in retail merchandising and propel them into the economic mainstream.

The men's group agreed to take this conversion on as their annual missions project. They immediately set about constructing a business plan, doing real estate research, studying traffic flow patterns—the kinds of things business types do in their sleep.

The men advised that the store should be on a bus line, be professionally merchandised and have a state-of-the-art cash register. It should have an advertising plan with regular sales and promotions. A full-time manager with retail experience was needed to run the operation. If we did it right, the store should break even within 24 months. These men understood business; we understood urban ministry. The combination seemed promising.

In fact, the plan worked better than we had projected. Eighteen months from opening day, the store (The Family Store as it was named) moved into the black and became a self-sustaining operation. We hired and trained unemployed community residents who were able to move into full-time jobs in the marketplace. The store's atmosphere was warm and inviting, a place customers felt good about visiting.

The greatest benefit, however, was the change in attitude between staff and community people that occurred. Customers felt valued rather than guarded against. They were needed and they sensed it. They were welcomed, not as subjects of compassion, but as essential customers. The store could not survive without them. Instead of staff expending energy on how to keep the customers' greed in check, the energy went into creating an atmosphere that would attract them. The music, the fragrance, the smiles, the attractiveness of displays, the neatness of racks, the courteous treatment—these became the agenda items of staff meetings. The dynamics of the relationship between the servers and the served changed dramatically.

This experience revealed that people—perhaps universally— would far rather engage in legitimate exchange than be the object of another's pity. There is something in one-way giving that erodes human dignity. This kind of compassion subtly communicates to the recipient "You have nothing of value that I desire in return." One-way mercy ministry, as kindhearted as the giver may be and as well intentioned, is an unmistakable form of put-down.

On the other hand, everyone loves to engage in the process of exchange. Everyone loves to find a bargain. There is something life affirming when someone comes to the bargaining table with a resource to barter. The playing field is leveled. The eyeing of each other's commodity takes place from both sides of the bargaining table.

Both sides have choice; both sides weigh the worth of the other's commodity. A deal is struck and an exchange is made. And remarkably, both parties leave the encounter feeling like they have gained more value than they brought.

THE MAGIC OF EXCHANGE

Remember your last garage sale? Or the last antique bargain you purchased at a flea market? Or the last car you traded? How is it that when a transaction is done well both purchaser and seller come away with a sense of gain? It's the magic of exchange. And it transcends the boundaries of age and gender, race and class. Whether the find is a rare Babe Ruth baseball card, a silk blouse reduced for quick sale or the perfect piece of land at the right price, the ecstasy of exchange is for all to enjoy.

Exchange is a remarkably invigorating process. The very thought of acquiring a new treasure motivates us to calculate value, rearrange priorities, juggle finances, analyze past performance and make predictions about the future. And ultimately, it pushes us to the risky edge of letting go of something valued in the hopes of gaining that which will be of greater worth to us.

However, when the labor you offer is unneeded in the marketplace or when your abilities are worth less to employers than the amount of your welfare check, you are exchange-less. Indeed, poverty may be defined as having little of value to exchange.

And when society subsidizes you for being a noncontributor, it has added insult to your already injured self-esteem.

From the time we insistently turned our heads away from our mothers' spoon-feeding to the day we left the nest, we have known instinctively that dependency is not for the healthy. How then have we created systems of dependency for those in need and thought it good? Or worse, established free clothes closets and food pantries devoid of the dignity of exchange and called it Christian?

The magic of exchange is part of God's common grace for all those He created in His image. The work of the Kingdom involves doing justice with and for those who have been excluded from the full measure of His grace. As co-creators with our Father, we have the high privilege and sober responsibility of re-creating systems that have fallen to self-interest, expediency and apathy. Ours is the task of modeling the highest forms of charity that include even the most vulnerable among us as valued participants.

Clothes closets can be converted to inner-city nearly-new shops, abundant with bargains. Proceeds will pay for overhead and create employment. Food pantries can become the sources for nonprofit grocery stores accessible to the poor who are paying exorbitant prices for food in their communities. Benevolence budgets can be turned into temporary employment funds to pay the needy for performing needed work. Our authentic transactions, governed by fairness and seasoned with generosity, will form the just and healthy ground between paternalistic charity and exploitation.

Consider the impact of such a system on an individual and the community where he lives. Watch as a young man enters The Family Store on a chilly overcast morning. He heads straight for the round chrome rack with a large "Sale—Reduced" sign on it. It is hanging full of a varied assortment of new and used winter coats. The young man looks at size and price tags, tries on several coats within his price range, then settles on a lined denim jacket that fits him comfortably. He brings it to the counter and hands the cashier a dollar. She smiles and asks if he wants a bag. He declines, slips on the jacket and walks out into the cold.

Keep your eye on that dollar. Watch as it is combined with the other sales receipts of the day and is reissued in the form of a paycheck to Betty, a trainee in retail merchandizing who works at The Family Store. Watch as Betty walks across the street after work to pick up her daughter at The Family Place preschool, which operates in the Presbyterian church. See her pay the sliding-scale tuition? Keep your eye on the dollar as it now passes into Connie's paycheck. Connie is a community resident who works at the daycare center. Follow Connie as she takes her own toddler down the street to the Grant Park Health Center to get her flu shots. The dollar moves again, this time in payment for healthcare treatment. It turns over into the paycheck of the clinic's secretary, Lou, who takes it over a few blocks to the Home Resource and Furniture Center and purchases a used crib for her new grandson. Joe, who has worked at the furniture center for three years—ever since he got out of a drug treatment program—helps Lou load the crib into her car. This sale, along with a hundred others, signals good business for the furniture center and that means job security for Joe. The dollar transfers again, this time into Joe's paycheck. After work, Joe stops into the Charis Community Housing office and makes his monthly payment on the affordable home he is buying for his family. The dollar is exchanged again. Charis buys a vacant lot with Joe's mortgage payment (combined with that of several other new homeowners) so that another house can be built for another family in the neighborhood.

The young man who bought the denim jacket has unwittingly set off an economic chain reaction that has in small but significant ways impacted the lives of a half-dozen people in his community. That dollar has turned over five, six, seven times, each time contributing to the economic vitality of the neighborhood. His money, spent and recycled among his neighbors, is a minute but powerful antidote to the devastating drain of dollars that plagues many poor communities.

Consider another scenario. The same young man enters a Bargain Store owned and operated by a national franchise headquartered out of state. He is delighted to find a warm coat that has been drastically reduced. With his dollar he makes a purchase. This time his dollar is divided between the store manager and the home office. The manager takes his share with him as he drives out of the neighborhood to his home in the suburbs. Headquarters divides the rest among employees and shareholders scattered across the country. The case can certainly be made that the Bargain Store serves the urban community by providing affordable clothes at good prices. And who would argue that a successful business enterprise is not good for the general economy? And what stockholder would complain about good earnings? But viewed through the lens of the community where the store is located, the Bargain Store has no positive economic impact save that of providing affordable products at a cheap price. It neither provides employment for local residents nor invests its profits in the local economy.

Unlike the first scenario where a dollar circulates several times within the community, each time enhancing the financial capacity of local enterprise as well as local residents, the Bargain Store removes money from the community. Although it does provide a product, at the same time it depletes community wealth.

Consider one more scenario—an even more familiar one. The young man enters a local church on a chilly winter morning and winds his way down a couple hallways to a room marked

"Clothes Closet." A volunteer greets him with a warm smile and invites him to look around. The young man finds where most of the coats are located and begins sorting through them—some on wire hangers, some stacked on folding tables, some still unpacked from the bags their donors delivered them in. He is delighted to find a warm denim work jacket in pretty good shape that fits him well. He sets it aside while he searches for another coat better suited for evening wear. The friendly volunteer points to the sign taped on the wall that reads, "One coat per customer please." The young man nods, picks up the denim jacket and exits the church.

End of scenario.

A gift has been given but there is no exchange. There is no economic benefit to the community, to *anyone* for that matter, except that the young man now has a warm coat on his back and his dollar still in his pocket. And that *is* something.

The Kingdom reserves a special place for the poor and for those who show compassion toward the poor. But how we demonstrate our compassion has everything to do with whether or not the poor actually feel valued. This is very good news indeed to Kingdom-minded people who are also bargain hunters, entrepreneurs, wheeler-dealers and creative types who know the magic of exchange. Ours is the unique opportunity to use our know-how and our creative energies to design methods of exchange that enable those with little as well as those with much to come to the table, participate in the excitement of making a deal and leave satisfied. With dignity intact.

As I mentioned earlier in this chapter, one of the inherent dangers of betterment programs is their tendency to erode human dignity. This became glaringly obvious to me the first Christmas I lived in the city. For a decade I had been engaged in urban ministry but had commuted daily from the suburbs. For several of those years, I had coordinated an adopt-a-family program at Christmas time. Urban families who had no money to buy gifts for their children were matched up with suburban families who had caring hearts and a surplus of material things. Our staff would provide the names, ages and sizes of the children and the addresses of the families.

On Christmas Eve day, the suburban families would deliver the gifts to their adopted family in the city. The spirit of the season as it was shared in this very personal and tangible way would enrich the lives of both poor and affluent families in unique ways. It was an idea that had great appeal and it gained momentum each year.

But the year I moved into the city, the first year I sat in living rooms with needy neighbors when the gift-bearing families arrived, I observed something I had never seen before. The children, of course, were all excited at the sight of all the colorfully wrapped presents. The mothers were gracious to their benefactors but seemed, to me at least, to be a bit reserved. If there was a father in the home, he simply vanished. At first sight of the gift-bearers, he disappeared out the back door. It dawned on me that something other than joyful Christmas sharing was happening here. Although the children were ecstatic, the recipient parents were struggling with a severe loss of pride. In their own homes, their impotence as providers was exposed before their children. The mothers would endure this indignity for the sake of their children, but it was often more than the fathers could take. Their failure as providers was laid bare. It was destroying what shreds of pride they were managing to hold on to.

It was obvious that this charity system had to change. The following Christmas, as caring people began to call in for their adopted city family, they were asked if they would be willing to give an extra gift this year. Would they give the gift of dignity to the dads? Instead of delivering the gifts directly to their adopted family, they were asked to bring them unwrapped to the Family Store where a Christmas toy shop would be set up.

A small price would be placed on each toy or article of clothing—somewhere between a garage sale and a wholesale price—and parents from the community would be invited in to Christmas shop. Those that had no money could work at the store to earn what they needed to purchase gifts for their family, since cash flow would be generated through the sale of the donations.

Then, on Christmas morning, parents in the city would experience the same joy as those in the suburbs: watching their children open the gifts they secured for them from the efforts of their own hands. We renamed the Adopt-a-Family program and called it Pride for Parents.

It was a quantum leap, selling donated gifts rather than the very personal and warm-feeling home-delivery method. But when we explained to donors what was happening to the dignity of their recipients, they could understand. They understood, too, that the extra gift that they were being called upon to give was that rush of joy they experienced at seeing the faces of children light up when the presents arrived. The Pride for Parents idea caught on and continues to grow each year. Toys are collected by churches, at office parties, by sponsoring corporations and by individual families who want their children to learn the importance of giving to others, especially those in need. And urban families by the hundreds stream into the Family Store excited to find wonderful "bargains." Some are put to work stocking shelves, unloading vans and sweeping up. Others put gifts in lay-away, paying a small amount each week until the full purchase price has been paid. The proceeds from the sale of donated toys is then used to hire and train unemployed parents throughout the year who will in time secure permanent, full-time employment that is sufficient enough to support their families. Thus the gifts at Christmas not only bring great joy during the holiday season but keep on giving all year long.

This process that we just discussed, of converting a better-ment program into a development program, is no simple mat-ter. It is far easier to run a free clothes closet out of a church basement than to start a retail clothing business that requires a suitable facility, professional staff, financial management systems, personnel policies, training manuals and so forth.

Even if we might all agree that a thrift store is a superior means for providing affordable clothing to needy families, the money required to launch it and the skill sets required to oper-ate it may feel too overwhelming to the compassion committee that has only a limited amount of time to volunteer. It is far easier to streamline a betterment program that serves people than to create a development system that empowers them.

Betterment is easier and it feels better. How heartwarming it feels to volunteer as a server for the Thanksgiving feast for the homeless! How right it feels collecting warm blankets to deliver to the shelter as a winter blast approaches! There is something in our spirits—something God-like—that causes our hearts to respond with compassion in the face of suffering and misfortune.

But as anyone will attest who has spent any extended time in such "mercy" activities, there is an ugly side that inevitably reveals itself. Greed, manipulation, a sense of entitlement, resentment—somehow these darker instincts are never far below the surface among the recipients of one-way charity. And even in the best of scenarios, when relationships between givers and receivers appear to be genuinely thankful and gracious, the ten-dency toward unhealthy dependency is ever-present.

A relationship founded on one's giving and the other's need never yields healthy outcomes. Even raising our own chil-dren teaches us that independence is the course toward which we must steer them if they are to become healthy, responsible adults. Love toward our children that does not require responsibility is pathological. It is no different in loving the poor.

If we are to rightly care for those in need, the responsibility lies with those with the resources to create systems of exchange built on interdependency rather than dependency. Though our hearts have compelled us to begin with compassionate betterment activities, we must engage our minds to move toward development. Benevolence funds become job banks. Clothes closets become thrift stores. Food pantries become food co-ops.

We get out of the business of giving away. We start using our heads as well as our hearts to build value into people and relationships—value realized only when authentic exchange occurs. Again, perhaps the greatest poverty of all is having nothing of value to offer the community. I want to believe that no one in my community is that poor.

CHAPTER 8

ON DOING GOOD

Feeding the hungry is the same as ministering directly to the Master. He counted it a measure of righteousness when He was hungry and we gave Him food (see Matt. 25:35). Soup kitchens for the homeless, food pantries for needy families, free turkeys at Thanksgiving . . . these expressions of care, then, must surely be the offerings to which our Lord was referring when He said, "Inasmuch as you did it to the least of these, my brethren, you did it to me" (Matt. 25:40).

How callous is the heart of one who would denigrate a free feast for the poor at Christmas. Or the delivery of food boxes to the doors of seniors in a high-rise. Critics might complain that sharing should not be limited to the holidays, but who would be so cold as to oppose it altogether?

John McKnight, that's who! Never do for others what they can do for themselves, is what he advises in his excellent book *Building Communities from the Inside Out.* To do for others what they can do for themselves is to make recipients the objects of our pity and deprive them of human dignity. Many other urban veterans agree. I am one of them.

This is not to say, of course, that those caught in dire straits— burned out of their home or starving from famine—should not be given aid. It does mean, however, that to provide free handouts to passive recipients without reasonable bootstrap expectations is to foster unhealthy dependency and promote an entitlement mentality.

I discover within myself two persistent temptations toward "doing for" the poor rather than "doing with" them. One is that it feels so good. To surprise a mother and her three little children with a bounty of good food at the very moment they have hit the bottom of the peanut butter jar produces a rush of warm feelings in the spirit that are deeply satisfying. Such an experience leaves little doubt that surely "it is more blessed to give than to receive" (Acts 20:35). The other temptation, and clearly the stronger one, is that it is much easier to do for people. It is so much quicker to drop change into a panhandler's Styrofoam cup than to learn his name and offer him work. Or to box up food in the church kitchen than to sit at the kitchen table of a needy family and work out a budgeting plan.

Does this mean then, that feel-good, easy charity is bad charity? I would not go that far. "Doing for" charity does meet a very basic human need, for the moment at least. Poorly nourished children certainly benefit from a nutritious meal delivered by a benevolent donor. And a homeless person whose stomach is filled with a hot meal from a soup kitchen may now use the coins in his cup to secure a shower and clean bed for the night (though who will ever know?). And who is to say if a needy recipient is in truth diminished in spirit by such giving? It would appear, on the surface at least, that donations are welcome.

One-way charity quite often elicits grateful responses and sometimes even pronouncements of God's blessings from beggars on the street. And what mother would not be genuinely appreciative for the unexpected provisions for her children? Yet, when one is struggling to survive, pride and dignity can be suppressed to a lower level on the hierarchy of human need.

"Doing for" charity can open a door into the world of human misery. It is a first step in understanding the overwhelming problems that can gain the upper hand on the less fortunate. It can open up one's heart and serve as catalyst for compassionate, redemptive involvement. It can change the life of both giver and recipient. Doing good can lead to doing what is best.

Take the Georgia Avenue Food Co-op, for example. (We'll take a closer look at this program later in the book.) A free Wednesday lunch at the Georgia Avenue Church for the poor of the community offered a forum where givers and recipients could sit at a table together. Over time recipients joined in as servers and clean-up workers and assisted with the sorting and distributing of foodstuff that was frequently donated. Under sensitive and creative pastoral leadership, a group of recipients organized themselves into a food cooperative, contributed modest bimonthly dues and leveraged their combined buying power to purchase substantial quantities of food from the Atlanta Food Bank. All of the functions of running the co-op—money collection, purchasing, transporting, distributing, bookkeeping, rule enforcement—were assumed by co-op members. When the group reached 30 households, a new co-op was created. Today there are four. Doing good can lead to doing what is best.

A food co-op owned and operated by the poor is certainly superior to a free lunch program, both in dignity and responsibility. A co-op, through the mutual efforts of participants, expands the food dollars of those whose incomes are meager. But a food co-op does not create wealth. It does not produce living-wage jobs in the community. It does not bring down the exorbitant prices that those without transportation must pay at convenience stores. Only a major food store can do this . . .

Like the one businessman Tom Cousins brought to East Lake in Atlanta's inner city. Captured by a vision to bring hope back to this despairing neighborhood, Tom converted the infamous "Little Vietnam" housing project into a safe, attractive, mixed-income apartment community. Mothers no longer had to sleep with their children behind barricaded doors. Drug dealers were rooted out and playgrounds became safe.

But those on limited incomes still paid twice as much for their groceries as those who could drive to the large stores several miles away. Using his considerable real estate experience, Tom approached the Publix chain and put together a deal sufficient to induce them to open a store directly across the street from the new Villages of East Lake apartments. Today, residents of East Lake enjoy what most Americans take for granted: the best food for the lowest cost of any nation on Earth. Even better, Publix has created scores of new, good-paying jobs for community residents.

But good can sometimes become the enemy of best. When our one-way giving becomes comfortable and our spirits are no longer stirred to find the deeper, more costly solutions, good has become the enemy of best. When our feeding programs value order and efficiency over the messiness of personal involvement, good has become the enemy of best. When recipients remain recipients and givers are content to remain givers, good has become the enemy of best.

Perhaps the best giving is the kind that enables the poor to know the blessedness of being givers.

CHAPTER 9

OCCUPYING THE HIGH GROUND

I stood on the glass strewn basketball court at the ruins of Jerome Jones School. I wished I were not alone. A growing circle of unsmiling faces stared at me, shifting in uneasy silence. It was only a matter of time until the confrontation would erupt.

The weapons that these people carried were neither guns nor knives. These were not street punks out to spill blood. They were sophisticated, moneyed professionals, who had secured their own personal pieces of urban real estate. And they were not about to yield an inch of their turf without a fight.

The tension had begun several months earlier when the vacant Jerome Jones School was being considered as a shelter for the homeless. The building had mysteriously caught fire and burned to a shell the week the school board was to render its decision. The board, desiring that the land be put to some positive use, offered it to our organization to be used as home sites for the poor.

Several yuppies who were renovating homes in the neighborhood challenged the school board's decision. They organized a political assault that pressured the board to rescind their contract with us. A sealed-bid auction would settle the matter. The highest offer would get the land. There were only two bidders—the yuppie group and FCS Urban Ministries (our community ministry). When the envelopes were opened and the bids were read, our offer was higher—by one dollar!

The conflict, though, was obviously not over. There were accusations of collusion with the school board and threats of legal action. Smear and fear tactics were employed to intimidate us. The outcry resounded throughout the community and reached as far as city hall. Nevertheless, the ownership of property was transferred to our organization.

Here on the basketball court was our first eye-to-eye, neighbor-to-neighbor face-off. The crowd had grown to 25 or more. I wondered if it contained one sympathetic member. The silence was finally broken. "Why do you want to ruin our community?" And with that a reservoir of stored-up emotions began to pour forth—anger, fear, resentment, outrage. These were high-stakes risk takers, pioneers who had staked out their claim on the urban frontier, and now their substantial investments were being threatened. These were not mean people. They were hard-working, self-respecting, even church-going folk.

They had nothing against the poor—they emphasized that again and again. It was just that affordable homes and more lower-income neighbors would hurt their property values. The necessary displacement of the poor from the community was an economic issue, not a moral one. No one wanted to be unkind, they assured me. They just wanted to build a good stable community.

I could see quite clearly that this was a classic battle between the spirit and mammon. These were people of good will whose hearts were torn between protecting their investments and caring for their neighbors in need. Either they could open places in their community and in their hearts for the less fortunate, thus risking lower appreciation of their homes, or they could choose profit as their preferred value and fight to protect their treasure. Of course it was a volatile, emotion-laden drama. On the broken concrete basketball court of a burnt-out school, ordinary, kind-hearted people stared at a painful choice. They were being forced to decide where they would commit their hearts—not just their treasures. This was at its most basic level a spiritual decision.

It was clear in my mind that I was occupying the moral high ground. I had not moved into the neighborhood for economic gain. I had come to identify with the plight of the vulnerable and to take up their cause. Building a block of small homes that low-income families could purchase without interest was an important step toward ensuring them a permanent place in the center of the community. There needed to be many more such houses, not fewer, I argued. It felt good to be standing firmly on the side of justice. Perhaps too good.

I listened to their pitiful pleas to at least reduce the number of small homes and make room for more market-rate housing. But I was in clear control of both the moral and legal high ground. I owned the land and I could do the right thing with it. And I would, I assured them.

It was not until two decades later that it dawned on me that my smug position on affordable housing was seriously flawed.

Katherine Grant, our new housing director, had been in the neighborhood less than a week when a rash of break-ins and rapes seized the community with terror. She had been very excited about moving into her new home, a restored Victorian on a lovely tree-lined street. But her enthusiasm was quickly overshadowed by grave concerns for her own safety. Instead of the creative joys of decorating and planting flowers, Katherine was consumed with urgency to install burglar bars, exterior lighting and an alarm system. She had expected to meet her neighbors at block parties and social events, not police-led crime-watch meetings.

Katherine understood community development. She lived much of her life in cross-cultural settings and had extensive urban real estate experience. And she was not one to passively sit by as a victim. She met immediately with the precinct captain to discuss strategies for community cooperation in apprehending the perpetrators. It was teenage gang activity, the police informed her.

They knew who three of the young thugs were and even where they lived—a couple blocks from Katherine on Grant Terrace. Grant Terrace . . . that had a vaguely familiar ring to it.

Back in the office she pulled the files on houses our ministry had built in the immediate area and to her dismay, many of the homes on Grant Terrace had indeed been built by our ministry. She immediately ordered police reports on all the addresses on Grant Terrace and the adjacent streets where we had built homes. The data that came back was deeply distressing. Much of the criminal activity and police incidents in recent years had been tracked back to our houses. And the police were hunting for one of the accused rapists who was from one of our families!

This harsh reality could not be farther from the original vision that inspired many caring volunteers to partner with us to construct these homes years ago. During those early days of our housing ministry, compassion for families in need of decent, affordable housing was the driving motivation behind our efforts. Building rows of modest homes on derelict land seemed so right. We simply did not know then what time and troubling experience was teaching us: Concentrating low-cost housing in a low-income area *reinforces* rather than *relieves* the pathology of poverty. Unfortunately, Katherine and her neighbors were reaping the bitter fruits of our flawed strategy.

Decisive, corrective action had to be undertaken. Families who were in violation of the law (which automatically placed them in violation of their mortgage or lease agreement) had to be evicted. Their homes had to be upgraded and sold to middle-income residents who embraced the values of community improvement. Organizing efforts had to be initiated to create block watches, streetscape improvements and code enforcement.

In short, we had to re-create in the neighborhood around Grant Terrace a healthy, self-sustaining, mixed-income community that supported a positive quality of life and that stimulated economic viability. Had I known two decades ago when I stood on the basketball court facing concerned neighbors what I know now, this volatile and costly remediation work would never have been necessary.

Mixed-income community development is not some romantic notion dreamed up by softhearted liberals. It is pragmatic strategy grounded in hard economic and social reality. After nearly four decades of failed social policies, our society has finally recognized that isolating people in poverty compounds is healthy neither for the poor nor for those who would avoid them. Thankfully, public housing policy has now shifted toward mixed-income development that affords the poor with quality-of-life standards and that models benefits of upwardly mobile neighbors. Cities are enacting "inclusionary zoning" ordinances to ensure that their workforce—their schoolteachers, secretaries, police, sanitation workers and other essential personnel—can live affordably in the city. Economically integrated communities, we are finally realizing, are healthy for the entire city.

In retrospect, it may not have been simply greed and materialism that stirred angry neighbors to gather on a glass-strewn ball court. They may have understood better than I that concentrating clusters of low-income housing was detrimental to both the affluent and the poor. Perhaps the mixed-income alternative that they advocated was the high road after all.

CHAPTER 10

THE PROBLEM OF PARKING

It was an ambush! There was no other way to describe it. We should have seen it coming when the private meeting in our City Council member's office was unexpectedly moved to a conference room. It was to have been a personal discussion with a pastor over a couple of vacant lots we owned adjacent to his church in South Atlanta. But when the room filled with several high-profile Atlanta ministers and three heavyweights from city council, it was apparent that this was going to be anything but a quiet, personal conversation.

Yes, we did own the land in question, we acknowledged. Yes, we did know that the church wanted the land for parking. These were lots we had acquired at the request of the community for building new homes, we explained. As a matter of fact, we owned a good number of lots in South Atlanta.

Eighteen months earlier, the neighborhood association, comprised mostly of senior homeowners, had appealed to our ministry to help them revitalize their badly deteriorated community. We agreed to partner with them. Together we designed a plan to rebuild dilapidated houses, construct new mixed-income housing, clean up trash-filled lots, and attract new homeowners back into the area. Key to implementing the plan was acquiring or gaining control of 200 vacant residential lots.

This ambush would have never happened had the church been part of the community the way it was in its younger years. There would have been no need. In those days the pastor and his family lived in the parsonage beside the church. Its members were neighbors who walked to church on Sunday mornings and

Wednesday evenings and for choir practice and youth fellowship. Parking then was a non-issue. But those days were long gone. The pastor and all but two of the members lived a good drive from the church. Any future growth would be dependent upon some younger preacher with enough charisma to draw in friends and acquaintances from around the city. Parking would thus be critical.

The aging pastor and his heir-apparent son wanted the lots next to the church. The future of the church, as they envisioned it, was dependent upon adequate parking. Though their current budget was insufficient to fix the leaking roof on their building, they clung tenaciously to the hope that better days lay ahead.

I was sympathetic to their plight. But more parking lots were not part of the community's plan. In fact, there was already far too much parking in the neighborhood. Two of the more successful churches had gobbled up entire blocks of land, land where houses once stood, land now blacktopped, sitting vacant six days out of seven. No, the community did not need more parking. It needed housing.

How strange it felt being in opposition to the church! But there we sat, lined up like infidels, facing the wrath of clergy and politicians. Johnny-come-lately's, we were being branded; white folk with no appreciation for the importance of the historic role of the black Church. It would be pointless to bring up our 30-plus years of serving the poor and, for sure, no one in this room was about to come to our defense.

It would do no good to explain that this church was no longer part of the community, or that parking lots were not community-friendly. Listening politely—that was our only recourse. Listen to the charges of insensitivity. Listen to the veiled threats. Listen to the guilt that was heaped upon our pagan heads.

The meeting ended with handshakes and smiles and an expressed confidence that we would do the right thing (which felt more like intimidation than a belief in our inherent goodness). In the final analysis, it would be the neighborhood's decision. After all, we were in South Atlanta at the invitation of the community and were simply implementing their plan. But just to cover our bases, we phoned our attorney to see what our legal standing was. To our astonishment, we learned that scores of similar incidents were erupting in cities all over the country. The Church in conflict with its community—it is apparently a sign of the times!

Something had gone very wrong. One might expect weird cults to ignite neighborhood controversy, but not traditional churches with long histories in their communities. I went to the Web and did a search of news articles and court cases on this issue. Our lawyer was right.

Cities were passing zoning ordinances to limit church growth, neighborhood groups were organizing against church encroachment into residential areas, citizens were filing for restraining orders to prevent churches from tearing down homes . . . and on and on and on. Claims and counter-claims, lawsuits and appeals, ministers condemning community opposition as satanic, neighbors fighting relentless religious forces that threatened to destroy the residential character of neighborhoods in the name of God.

It was very difficult to determine who was wearing the white or black hats here. These were all good people but with terribly different perspectives. *Must I choose one side over the other*, I wondered. *Perhaps there is a way to make lemonade out of this lemon of a dilemma.* The Church could ask itself what kind of reorientation would be required to make it community-friendly once again. And the neighborhood could ask itself what kind of community planning would include the Church as a central player.

It may have been unrealistic for the Church to limit its membership and outreach to its immediate parish, but at least the pastor could live in the neighborhood and become active in the neighborhood association. And the community could provide a prime lot for the building of his home.

The Church could promote community development efforts by recruiting strong, faith-motivated families to move back into the area to re-neighbor it. And the neighborhood could attract building partners to provide special financing and down-payment assistance for families that the Church would pre-qualify. The Church could start a tutoring program for neighborhood children and the community could mobilize volunteer tutors and fundraising events to support it. And a parking lot could double as a basketball court.

These are all good ideas. But only two things are certain: A community devoid of the influence of the Church will surely suffer from a lack of spiritual vitality. And a church alienated from the people who live around it can hardly bear faithful witness to its creed. But who is willing to make the first move?

CHAPTER 11

SERVANTS OR FRIENDS?

Jesus had it backward.[1] He was always turning things upside down. The poor, not the rich, would inherit the Kingdom. The hungry would be the ones who in the end would be satisfied. He was always inverting things like this. He told His eager, ambitious followers that servanthood, not leadership ability, was the measure of greatness in God's order of things. "The greatest among you will be your servant," He declared (Matt. 23:10-12, *NIV*).

And so it would be. Those who followed Him would become known as Christ-ones, the people who had it backward. Their highest vision of the Christian purpose would be to reverse the order and fulfill a mission of service. They would follow the example of their Servant-leader and wash each other's feet. They would serve rather than rule—act as servants rather than lords.

Over time, however, a problem developed with their dedication to Christian service. The Crusaders, in their zeal to convert, thought they were servants of Christ. And likewise the Conquistadors. But they really didn't have the backward thing down. Like many others who are zealous for right causes, they used the idea of servanthood to conquer, rule and dominate others in Christ's name.

They had Christ backward. It is not enough, therefore, to ask whether someone says he or she is serving Christ. There are bad servants as well as good servants. The critical issue may be in understanding the difference. A good servant must really have it backward. He can't use the imperatives of mission and service to dominate and control.

Today it seems much easier to distinguish the good servants from the bad. The media helps us make that distinction. Bad servants are crooked politicians, profiteers who use friendship to separate seniors from their savings, and preachers who fleece their flocks for personal gain.

But our good servants seem to clearly help, care and cure rather than conquer, exploit and control. They are doctors, teachers, social workers, professors, lawyers, ministers—the professionals who serve. Our society has even made these good servants, the helping professionals, the economic base of the nation. In GNP terms, nearly two-thirds of our employed people now produce service. We have become an economy of servants. Instead of a nation of conquistadors, we are a nation of servers.

As Christians we could celebrate the institutionalization of the good servant. Ours is finally a society of caring, helping, curing servanthood. We laud the value of professional servanthood and pay for it generously. It would be interesting to know, however, what Christ might see in our society of servants, given His tendency toward getting things backward. Would He still have it backward? Would He even reject a society of good servants?

The answer is, probably not, unless He saw good servants becoming lords. Probably not, unless He saw help becoming control or care becoming commercialized. On the other hand, if He found servants caught up in commercialized systems of control, He would certainly insist that we still didn't get it—that our servanthood had become lordship. The question, then, is whether we are a nation of good servants or lords of commercialized systems of service that attempt to exert control.

I wonder if the reality of humanness will always make servanthood into lordship. It may be that there is no way to define service in order to keep from making it a system of control. With all our Christian devotion to the idea of service, could it be that service is an inadequate ideal, a value so easily corrupted that we should question its usefulness?

At the Last Supper, Christ was telling the disciples those things of greatest importance. It was His final opportunity to communicate the central values of the faith. "No longer do I call you servants," He said, "for a servant does not know what his master is doing; but I have called you friends, for all things that I heard from My Father, I have made known to you" (John 15:15).

Finally, Christ said you are not servants. You know the Father's heart. You know the inside story. You are friends.

Perhaps beyond the revolutionary Christian mandate of service is the final revolution, the possibility of being friends. Friends are people who know each other, who care, respect, struggle and are committed through time. Christ's mandate to be friends is a revolutionary idea in our serving society.

Why friends rather than servants? Perhaps it is because He knew that servants could always become lords but that friends could not. Professional servants may operate on the assumption that "you will be better because I know better," but friends believe that "we will be better because we share in each others' lives." Servants are people who know the mysteries that can control those to whom they give "help." Friends, on the other hand, are free to give and receive help from each other.

Here we are, a nation of professional servers, following Christ's mandate to serve. And here He is, at the final moment, getting it backward once again. The final message is not to serve. Rather, He directs us to be friends.

Note
1. This chapter is adapted from the essay "On the Backwardness of Prophets" in John McKnight's penetrating book *The Careless Society-Community and Its Counterfeits* (New York: Basic Books, 1995).

PART III

TOWARD RESPONSIBLE CHARITY

Everyone must pull his own weight. That is the key to responsible charity—which is not to say that everyone has equal capacity—just equal responsibility. When individuals, like communities, assume responsibility for their own destiny, when they abandon self-pity, self-indulgence and blame to face the hard work of building (or rebuilding) their lives, they have taken a giant step toward health. Obviously, no man is an island. Everyone needs others on the path toward becoming all that we were created to be. It is the nature of those relationships that will determine whether we emerge as strong, contributing members of the community or whether we become victims who blame others for our problems.

In this section we will look at people, programs and neighborhoods that are feeling their way toward responsible participation in the larger human community. It is a long journey from softhearted, one-way charity to reciprocal, interdependent relationships. The road map that shows us how to navigate our way from prideless dependency systems to dignity-enhancing systems of exchange is not yet charted. But there are those pioneers who are forging their way into this territory. The intelligence they are gathering is instructive.

CHAPTER 12

ON CARE AND
ACCOUNTABILITY

Not everyone is equal. I think it is okay to say that now. Certainly we are all of special worth in the eyes of our Creator and we do have equal rights under the U.S. Constitution. But we are not all equal. Even a child can see that.

Our intelligence differs widely. Some of us have multiple gifts and others of us are single-talent people. Some are born leaders; others are natural followers. Some have outgoing personalities that propel them into high-profile roles, while others are more introverted and behind the scenes. Some people are born with brains, good looks and charm; some are homely and dull. Some people are born with deficits; some are born *into* deficits. Some will squander their privilege, while others will capitalize on every opportunity. Some will overcome daunting disadvantages, while others will sink into blame and self-pity.

But why do I belabor the point? Because the time has finally arrived when we can venture out from behind our timidity and admit to ourselves that inequities are not necessarily the same as injustices—which is in no way to minimize the damaging effects of injustice. To be sure, many inequities are created by human malevolence, but many more, perhaps most, are not.

To pretend that, given equal opportunity, all people could do equally well is a romantic and altogether unhelpful notion. Our hearts may desire it to be so and political correctness may keep us from publicly saying otherwise, but kindhearted denial is hardly a kindness. We are equal neither in *capacity* nor *potential*. We are equal only in *responsibility*.

Of course, there will always be those among us who must rely on the responsibility of others—infants, Alzheimer's patients, the severely brain-damaged. But for the rest of us, we are responsible to do the best with the uneven hands we have been dealt. Remove this personal accountability and atrophy of the spirit sets in.

Anyone who has been in the helping professions for any length of time will readily admit that you can't fix people. Nothing is more disheartening than to invest enormous amounts of compassion and energy in counseling, treating, training and connecting an addicted person only to have him throw it all away by returning to his destructive patterns. No amount of supervision or intense support can produce moral character in another. It is only when one is ready to take responsibility for his own life and face the daily discipline of right decision making that support becomes beneficial. It is true with all of life. When we do for others what they can do for themselves, we cripple them.

"Easy for you to say," I hear the retort of one beset by adversity. "Easy to preach responsibility to others when you've been born into privilege." I must concede that one who has life easy, who has been shaped by the security of loving parents and blessed with a comfortable livelihood, can hardly relate to the powerlessness of the broken whose best efforts are insufficient to lift them above bare survival. But to whom much has been given much is required. The strong and well bear the greater weight for care.

Which is not to say that one whom life has shortchanged is exempted from pulling his or her weight, as well as lending a hand to other struggling souls. Both achiever and survivor share a common responsibility: to make the most of their unequal lots in life.

Empowerment is a popular word these days; however, it may be a misnomer. People, like butterflies, have an inbred capacity to emerge into creatures of unique beauty. But intervene in the chrysalis process when the caterpillar is undergoing its transformation and the process may be aborted. Assist the emerging butterfly as it struggles to break out of its cocoon and it may never develop the strength to fly. We may protect the cocoon from predators, even shield it from winter's hostile blast, but do more than create the conditions for timely emergence and we will cause damage. Thus, people, like butterflies, cannot be empowered. They will emerge toward their uniquely created potential, given an environment conducive to success.

How then do we care for those in need without doing them harm? Social policies over the past four decades have taught us that programs intended to help can rather quickly become entitlements, and entitlements engender unhealthy dependency. Our challenge, then, is to couple unconditional kindness with appropriate opportunities that foster one's growth toward full potential. The gestation time will vary widely. Some will surprise us with their strength and quickness. Others will disappoint us with their lack of motivation and slowness. But all must assume full responsibility for their own rate of progress or regress. We who would help do a disservice by offering relief from the essential discipline of their emergence from the cocoon.

CHAPTER 13

GOING DEEPER WITH DEVELOPMENT

The old adage goes: Feed a man a fish and he'll eat for a day; teach him to fish and he'll eat for a lifetime. But suppose that man who we have taught to be a proficient fisherman comes home one day with an empty stringer? The pond, he announces, has been fished out—overfished. There have been just too many fishermen taking fish from the pond. All the edible-size fish have been caught.

In order for the fisherman to continue to feed himself and his family, he will have to leave and search for other ponds—unless, of course, we decide to take some corrective action and find a way to restock the pond. That would require us to shift our ministry emphasis from teaching men to fish to emphasizing environmental conservation. This would represent a change in strategy at least as dramatic as the original shift we took when we decided to get out of our feeding program and start the fishing school.

In those wonderful early years when we at FCS Urban Ministries spent our days feeding the hungry, we felt so close to God's heart, so clearly obeying Christ's command to directly care for the least of these. There was something so uncomplicated and pure about that ministry. That was before the nagging realization dawned on us that we might actually be fostering dependency among the hungry we were feeding.

Our desire to do good had unintended consequences, and so, in order to be responsible as well as caring, we made the decision to scale back our hands-on feeding program and instead help the hungry learn to feed themselves. We decided to teach people how to fish.

Training fishermen to catch their own food had its own rewards, though we surely missed the warm feelings of placing food into a man's outstretched hand. Graduation day from the fishing school was inspiring, and there was great satisfaction in seeing our trainees return home with stringers full of fish they had caught.

But then we were confronted with yet another unintended consequence of our ministry. We had not considered that the pond would be unable to meet the demands of so many of our graduates. We had produced some fine fishermen, but we were about to lose them from our community because they could no longer sustain themselves. What was good for individuals was proving to be hurtful to our community. Unless, once again, we altered our mission and did something about the deteriorating environmental concern.

Of course, it would certainly have been legitimate ministry if we'd decided to stay the course and remain focused on what we do best—training fishermen. We could have continued to give our students the skills they needed to make it on their own. We might have even added a course to our curriculum on finding plentiful ponds, streams and lakes out in the larger world. Who knows, we might have produced some world-class fishermen who could come back to our school as chapel speakers from time to time and inspire our students by stories of enormous fish they have caught.

But if we wanted to be responsible to both our graduates and to our community, we would have to devote at least some of our time to improving the environment. And as we pondered how we might go about this, we realized that we did in fact have a couple of well-connected friends in the state fish-hatchery industry. Also, we knew of several foundations that funded conservation initiatives.

We decided it was worth a try. With surprisingly little effort, we explained our dilemma to our fish-hatchery friends, wrote proposals and received start-up grants from a couple of foundations, and along with a crowd of excited neighbors witnessed the release of thousands of fish into the community pond. Our fishermen were back to work!

It has been quite a journey since then. We began with individual betterment (feeding a man a fish), shifted to individual development (teaching him to fish), and then moved into community betterment (restocking the pond). But the journey was not over.

By the time we restocked the pond for three seasons and were writing our fourth round of grant proposals, it became apparent that we were emerging as the major source of the community's food supply. When the pond became depleted, our graduates came to us to restock it. It became an expectation that felt uncomfortably like an entitlement. We felt caught between having to institute control measures on the pond—quotas and limits—or expand our fundraising efforts to keep up with a growing demand for free fish.

Neither alternative was very attractive. In an unexpected twist, we found ourselves in much the same place as we were when we first began our feeding ministry—creating unhealthy dependency among those we felt called to serve.

Yet another shift was called for—a shift from community betterment to community development. Just like training our men to fish for themselves, we needed to enable our community to take responsibility for its own food supply. Organizing a community development corporation (CDC) and teaching residents how to write grant proposals was one possible approach. But there was a better way. If the community bought the pond, it could harness the local fishing industry and create additional enterprise.

If the community owned the pond, it could charge a reasonable fee for fishing, which could be used to keep the pond well-stocked without outside grant support. It could set up a cannery that buys fish from local fishermen and hires community residents to clean, pack and ship fresh fish to other markets. The community, with this kind of sound business plan, could secure loans and attract investors, which would give it respect and equal standing in the mainstream economy.

The progression from betterment toward development is a natural one, assuming we do not lock in our programs and get stuck in one mode. A similar progression is from individual toward community. Graphically it might look like this:

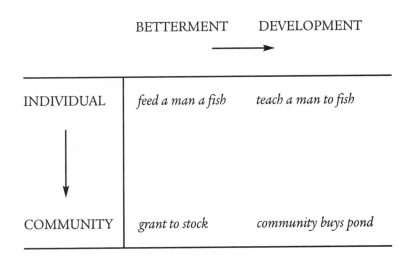

	BETTERMENT	DEVELOPMENT
INDIVIDUAL	*feed a man a fish*	*teach a man to fish*
COMMUNITY	*grant to stock*	*community buys pond*

Have we carried our analogy too far? Let's hold some real-life experience up against it and see if it holds true. The old Georgia Avenue Presbyterian Church, just down the street from our new inner-city Atlanta home, had closed down. For nearly a century it had been a beacon of light in the Grant Park neighborhood, but its aging membership had moved away and simply did not have the energy or resources to keep the Sunday worship and community outreach programs going. With great sorrow they had a funeral service for the church and Georgia Avenue Presbyterian Church ceased to be.

The church had been locked up for two years when we made the decision to move our family and ministry offices into Grant Park. The location, just a block from the home we had built, seemed like an ideal spot to house our ministry. So we appealed to the presbytery, which had taken responsibility for the vacant property, to allow us to reestablish ministry and start a worshiping fellowship there. They agreed, and soon the church was alive again with all sorts of activities.

Because the church historically had offered programs for the poor of the area, we soon had visitors from the community asking for food and clothes and rent money. Quite naturally, we wanted to be responsive to the needs of the neighborhood, so we immediately set about establishing a clothes closet and a food pantry.

A Wednesday noon meal for the community, prepared and served by partner churches, had been part of the church's tradition, so we renewed this program. It was not at all difficult to restock the food pantry—we merely had to ask our supporting churches to do regular food collections. Then when families ran out of food before their checks arrived, we could offer them boxes of canned goods and cereal to last them through the month.

Over time, our faithful volunteers who sacrificially gave of their time to prepare and serve hot meals and clean up afterward began to ask if the people they served ever got jobs and moved out of poverty. These same people, they observed, were in the food line every week and had been for many months.

Besides, the lines were growing and the quantity of food being consumed was increasing.

Was this really helping the poor to get on their feet or was it fostering dependency? The very least they could do was clean up after themselves, the volunteers commented, though not wanting to complain. And that's how the shift toward development first began. The recipients were invited to help with dishes, wipe tables and mop the floors—duties they readily volunteered to assume. Those waiting for groceries were asked to fill the boxes with a balanced assortment and assist in passing them out. Interestingly, those who picked up these responsibilities began to enforce a level of accountability among their peers—no seconds until everyone has eaten, everyone puts their silverware in the soapy water, only one box per family and single men don't need a whole box. The more ownership they were given, the more accountability they exercised and the less the staff and suburban volunteers felt presumed upon.

Although the sharing of responsibilities felt like a step in the right direction, the ministry was still a free food program that did little to encourage the poor toward self-sufficiency. Yet the system was working quite well, the volunteers seemed willing enough to prepare and serve food indefinitely, and churches were more than pleased to include food drives as a regular event on their missions calendar. And so it continued for years. Until one day, our pastor, weary of processing endless streams of donated food and exasperated by surly crowds of complaining people, came up with an idea.

What if recipients were offered membership in a food co-op where they invested a small portion of their own money, elected a representative to make a run to the city food bank to purchase (by the pound) a weekly supply of surplus food, and distributed that food among themselves? For three dollars each member could receive at least 30 dollars worth of food.

Co-op members could decide what food they wanted and instruct their driver to look for bargains but avoid overloading them with too much of one thing. They might even be able to get a little grant money to launch the idea, maybe even purchase a used pickup truck to make the food-bank runs.

The response was tentative at first. It was so much simpler to just show up at church and get your free food. But a handful of folks were interested enough to attend a planning meeting to discuss the idea further. And as they explored the benefits of the concept and saw how their grocery dollars could be multiplied, their excitement grew.

At first a dozen, then two-dozen decided to take the risk. They signed a membership commitment to invest regularly and perform their share of co-op responsibilities, put their first three dollars into the kitty, and sent their representatives off to the food bank in the pastor's car. The first distribution was abundant.

As co-op members told their friends, the concept began to catch on. The first co-op closed its membership at 30—a number that proved through trial and error to be manageable. A second was started. Then a third. Each co-op became a community within itself with elected officers, a treasurer, a driver and distribution committees. For some members it became like their church, where they could pray together and share joys and concerns. The pride of ownership, of self-management, of securing for themselves their own food (even though it was from a surplus source) yielded a respect that was noticeably absent from our free food system. There was no going back.

With minimal outside support, the co-ops became self-sustaining. They did, with the pastor's assistance, secure a grant from a local foundation that enabled them to purchase a truck that all three groups used for food pickup and delivery. Food sorting and boxing became their weekly social hour at the church, where they shared stories, personal concerns and recipes.

One co-op discovered that among its members there was considerable cooking talent. This was enthusiastically confirmed by tasty dishes they prepared and brought to share with the group. "We should start a restaurant," one member exclaimed after finishing a piece of delicious sweet potato pie that a fellow member had baked. The comment ignited a lively discussion. One said she had always wanted to own a restaurant. People would come from miles around for that sweet potato pie, another complimented. Another said he had a killer recipe for ribs. Was this idea really possible? They would ask the pastor.

Over the next few months, the pastor and co-op members explored the feasibility of starting a community restaurant. It would require much more than cooking talent. They would have to secure a suitable building, outfit a commercial kitchen that would meet county health codes, buy all the tables, chairs, dishes, utensils, cash register . . . the list went on and on. It was overwhelming, really. The amount of time and money it would require just to set up a restaurant was mind-boggling.

The pastor assured them that if they were serious about this he would help them find investors and others in the restaurant business that would consult with them. It was the most exciting vision any of them had ever dreamed about, and the biggest one for sure.

It took more than a year of diligent study, real estate research, proposal writing, selling investors, securing loans, signing contracts and remodeling an old storefront within sight of the Atlanta Braves baseball stadium before the grand opening of Tummy and Soul was announced. As their first customers filed in, the co-op members were smiling from ear to ear. They had done it! They had turned a vision into reality. They had a business of their own.

The journey from betterment to development is neither smooth nor easy. But when we compare the expressions on the faces of those jostling in the free food line with those bussing tables and sweating over the stove at Tummy and Soul, there will remain no question in our minds as to which approach is better. Look deeply into the eyes of the poor and let what you see determine the approach you take in ministry. Dignity, not pity, will win every time.

Chapter 14

SO YOU WANT TO CHANGE A BAD NEIGHBORHOOD, DO YOU?

Bad neighborhoods—what can we do about them? Respectable parents warn their children to steer clear of them. Slumlords collect rents from them. Politicians make promises to clean them up. Rich kids in BMWs sneak into them to purchase drugs. Elected officials argue over how much of the city budget should be spent on them. Police patrol them. Teachers try to inspire students to get out of them.

Publicly, we all say that we want to see bad neighborhoods transformed into healthy places for children to grow up. And that can certainly happen. But first we have to get honest with each other. Do we really want to see change? Badly enough to take some heat? Let's see.

First, though, let's look at some of the questions that might start potential volunteers and ministry leaders thinking about whether or not they are really committed to seeing change in inner-city locations.

10 QUESTIONS VOLUNTEERS/DONORS WANT TO ASK MINISTRIES BUT SELDOM DO

Serving is a tricky business. It sounds very heartwarming and loving when the minister tells us about a neglected child who needs someone to cuddle her or a homeless man who needs a warm blanket to insulate him from the cold winter winds. Our hearts leap to meet human need. We sign up enthusiastically to volunteer, eager to serve our Lord, ready to obey His commands to touch and be touched by those in need. But once the initial emotional rush has calmed and the realities of our busy schedules and time commitments are calculated, certain questions inevitably arise—questions we would like to ask of the ones who are in charge of the ministry we will be serving with, questions we are generally far too polite to ask. Regardless of the task we volunteer for—whether high-touch personal involvement or hands-on labor or joining a nonprofit board or making a donation—we wish we had a way of knowing a few important things about the ministry. Perhaps stating some of those questions will help to open a delicate discussion.

1. *Will my investment make any real difference?* How will I know? How can I be assured that my involvement is having any significant impact on the lives of those I am serving? Are there any measurable outcomes, any benchmarks for tracking real change?

2. *Am I really helping or is this just to make me feel good?* Is this project just make-work to give my church group and me an "urban experience"? Is this more about an awareness-raising adventure for us or is this mission project really going to make a positive difference in the lives of the poor?

3. *Will this be a personally meaningful experience?* Will this work touch my heart, open my eyes, show me Jesus' compassion in new ways and change my life? Please tell me that it is about more than just fellowship with my friends.

4. *Does this ministry really get at the root causes?* Is it a band-aid approach or is it major surgery? Serving food at the soup kitchen may keep people from starving but are you doing anything to help people deal with their addictions, their joblessness? Does your organization attempt to get at the underlying issues that cause poverty?

5. *Will you value my time?* Will you have someone there to meet us, give us a concise orientation, give us clear instructions, put us right to work, have the tools and equipment ready? Will you make efficient use of my time so that I don't feel like I'm wasting my day standing around waiting?

6. *Do you just want my money or do you really want me involved?* Do you actually need more volunteers to accomplish your mission or is this a public relations tour to sell me on your program? Are you creating work for me to do as a means of getting my buy-in? If you had the choice, would you take my money or me?

7. *Is the ministry cost-effective?* Do you get good results from the dollars expended and how do you measure those outcomes? Do you measure activity or impact? Number of participants or number of successes? And what is success? Do you have an annual audit?

8. *Are you open to change if I offer solutions or improvements?* Do you really want my involvement? Do you want my insights for your work, even if it means changing some of the ways you are doing business?

9. *Will you deal with me responsibly and follow through on your commitments?* Can I count on you to return phone calls promptly and send requested information in a timely manner? Will you keep appointments and be up-front with me about what I can expect from you?

10. *Will I get feedback on how the mission is going?* Will you send me a report on the outcome of our project? Will you send me personal acknowledgements when I make donations? Will you send me periodic updates on your work?

10 QUESTIONS MINISTRIES WANT TO ASK VOLUNTEERS/DONORS BUT SELDOM DO

Clearly, the very best way for a ministry to capture the interest and secure the commitment of supporting friends is to involve them in front-line, hands-on work in "the trenches." While some ministries are largely volunteer-driven, most use volunteers to supplement the work of paid staff. And because volunteers provide some of the most fertile fundraising ground to till, there is often some mix of motives about whether the volunteers' work or their money is most needed. When an organization's survival rests on the good will and contributions of supporters, however, it is likely to steer clear of any such discussions—or any topics, for that matter, that might tend to alienate its constituents. Thus, seldom voiced but often felt are the following questions on the minds of most or all nonprofit staff who coordinate volunteer groups.

1. *How much staff time will it consume to put you to work?* How much of our ministry energy will have to be

diverted away from our mission to prepare for, arrange food and lodging for, line up work sites for, develop training materials for and entertain your group? Is this a good trade-off?

2. *Will your volunteering cost us more than it is worth?* Will the time and effort we expend on hosting you translate into greater productivity and effectiveness in our mission than if you had not come and we did the ministry ourselves? Is it more bother than it's worth?

3. *Will the ministry actually get any money from you?* In addition to your food and transportation expenses, will you bring with you the materials needed for the program? Will you compensate us for the wear and tear on our facility and the cost of utilities and management?

4. *How much will hosting you pull us away from our mission?* Our primary mission is caring for the poor, not raising awareness of suburban youth groups. Our work is building redemptive relationships with the disenfranchised, not team-building for church groups. Will you provide your own leadership, supervision, training and support for your volunteers?

5. *Is this about you having a meaningful experience or about serving the poor?* I understand the importance of life-changing experiences, of exposing your children to a world of need, but is serving others really about *you*?

6. *Will you share your contacts /networks with us?* As you see the needs, will you connect us with others who

can help us have greater impact? Will you introduce us to new friends who can support the ministry? Will you help us share the vision?

7. *Are you more concerned with measurable results than being faithful?* Quick fixes generally don't last. Poverty develops over generations and it will take time—decades perhaps to undo its effects. Immediate results are wonderful, but long-term commitment will win the day. Can you live with sporadic and incremental changes?

8. *What is your agenda, really?* No one's motives are entirely pure, but . . . Is this about garnering good PR for your company? Are you feeling pressure from your church to develop a great missions program? Is this a "should" or "ought" that you got from a sermon? I can deal with these—it would just help if I knew.

9. *Can you serve without feeling the need to take over?* Can you adjust your expectations to allow for a more laid-back management style? Can you subordinate your substantial abilities to indigenous leadership that may be less proficient?

10. *Will you attempt to control me with your money?* Does your gift have strings? What are they?

Once you've addressed these questions it's time to get into the real stuff involved in volunteering and in ministries that desire to change a bad neighborhood. First we will have to get past the romantic notion that neglected communities must be empowered to rebuild themselves from within. Some advocates preach that it is disrespectful for outsiders to initiate change, that somehow this diminishes the dignity of existing residents. In truth, ignoring a community and allowing it to degenerate into a ghetto is far more demeaning and insensitive than imposing positive changes.

Certainly, residents must be taken into account, communicated with and invited into the planning process. But we must be honest enough to acknowledge that the expertise, resources and connections essential for the revitalization of a deteriorated neighborhood have long ago departed. Mega-doses of outside energy and leadership will be required to turn a blighted area around. The process of change should be respectful, but it will not come without causing disruption. Change is always difficult and often painful. Even so, the commitment to change must not subordinate itself to the whims of neighborhood politics or to the rhetoric of outspoken, nay-saying activists.

Is the city ready? Is there a corporate will to refocus public dollars, enforce building codes, commit to planning staff time, reallocate police presence, apply for grants, enter into partnerships with the private sector, create new land uses, oppose slumlords and face controversy? If there is a sufficiently strong consensus among city council members and community leaders to lock arms and put their combined energies behind the venture, the odds of success will increase dramatically.

Who is the visionary? Without a vision, the people perish, said the prophet of old. Has a vision for community transformation been growing large in the spirit of some leadership-type person? There is a very big difference between a vision and a bright idea. Good ideas are a dime a dozen. They are the staple of entrepreneurs and creative people. And many good things come of bright ideas.

A compelling vision, though, has a magnetic quality about it. It draws people and their resources around it. Coincidences converge. People are inspired. Magic happens. But a vision must be both communicated and managed—thus the crucial role of the visionary. The visionary is both the spokesperson and the guardian of the vision. The visionary stays the course, keeps the project from getting sidetracked by diversionary issues, and protects it from being dissipated by too broad a focus. His or her role is more of a calling than a job. City and neighborhood support are important; committees and task forces and boards are necessary; but a visionary is essential.

Does the vision make good business sense? As important as renovated houses, good youth programs, better trash pick-up and stepped up policing may be, such treatments do not address the underlying sources of pathology that cause communities to deteriorate. Neighborhoods decline because of disinvestment. Homeowners move away, landlords defer maintenance, the quality of life declines, property values depreciate, legitimate businesses leave and illegitimate enterprise fills the void.

Loading up a depressed neighborhood with services—faith-based or otherwise—does nothing to reverse that downward spiral. As a matter of fact, concentrating social services can actually draw more needy recipients into an area—hardly a good community-development strategy. Reinvestment is needed. Bottom line: The community must be re-neighbored. While it is important to preserve (and create) affordable housing options for existing low-income residents, strategies to attract middle-income neighbors back into the area are essential.

Urban pioneers, propelled by their hearts rather than investment opportunity, can lead the way. But it is the charming streetscapes, restored bungalows, clustered town homes around private courtyards, loft apartments—the familiar handiwork of real estate developers—that will draw young professionals (and their resources) back to the neighborhood. A community will never come back to life through subsidies and services. Economic viability is the only thing that will build and sustain a healthy community.

And then there is the whole issue of the spiritual health of the neighborhood. Community rebirth is different from personal regeneration, which can enable individuals to rise above the destructive influences of their environment. Community rebirth transforms the seedbed of pathology. But that's a later discussion. It's a matter of triage. We've got to stop the bleeding first.

CHAPTER 15

MAKING THE NEIGHBORHOOD WORK

"You need a job!" Our 16-year-old son, Jonathan, was already bored and summer vacation had scarcely begun. The adventures that some of his north side school friends were planning all required money—money that he didn't have and that we were not prepared to shell out. The kid needed a job. I told him so.

"I'm going over to the zoo," he finally conceded after it was apparent that he was going to have to fund his own summer fun. Zoo Atlanta is a short walk from our house. They don't pay much but do provide their employees with sharp uniforms and safari pith helmets. It was a wholesome environment for young people, so we were pleased at Jonathan's decision.

Unbeknown to him, we knew one of the senior staff there, who we immediately called to alert for Jon's arrival. "No special favors," we insisted. But it came as no great surprise that Jonathan was immediately hired.

With money in his pocket, Jonathan could afford gas for our old Suburban, which became a rolling party packed full of frolicking school friends. On his off-work hours when he was not driving around town, you could find him down the street shooting hoops at the neighborhood basketball court. Some of his friends, particularly those from lower-income families, had more time on their hands than money in their pockets—a predicament the zoo had remedied for Jonathan. "They're hiring at the zoo," he told his unemployed buddies. "Put me down as a reference." In no time five of his friends had jobs at the zoo.

We did not need a youth employment program in our neighborhood that summer. Nor the next. Or next. We had connected neighbors. We learned that if neighbors who had contacts were merely willing to share those contacts, willing to use their "insider" status to open a door for their neighbors, a funded and staffed job program was unnecessary. The same was true for adults. Those with good paying positions in stable companies had only to share the job openings posted on their bulletin boards in order for new and better opportunities to open up for their underemployed neighbors. Good neighbors are preferable to good programs any day. And they're a whole lot cheaper.

The better our street functioned as a community, the less we seemed to need the support of externally funded programs. Take teen pregnancy, for example. The number of teenage girls in Georgia who become pregnant out of wedlock is epidemic. It is even worse in Atlanta. We have a lot of young girls on our street, most from single parent homes. Yet the rate of pregnancy among them is well below the *national* average (not to speak of Georgia). That's not because we have a teen pregnancy prevention program. It's because neighbors have made the commitment to keep an eye open for potential problems. More teenage girls conceive during the hours of 4 to 7 P.M. than any other time of the day (so says a Health and Human Services report). These are the most unsupervised hours when kids are out of school and parents are still at work.

One day while I was home from work in the midmorning, I glanced out the front window and saw our 15-year-old neighbor, Pamela, walking past with a male friend. I mentioned it to my wife, who reminded me that we had committed with our neighbors to notify parents if we observed friends coming by their homes when they were at work. We debated for a few moments about who should make the phone call. I lost. Somewhat reluctantly I pulled out the neighborhood directory and dialed the number. Pamela answered. I asked to speak to her mother. Not home. I asked for her dad but, of course, he was not home either. Was she home sick today? I probed in an innocent voice. No, Pamela fumbled, she had come home to, uh, pick up a book. I asked for her father's work number and hung up.

"Dave, I don't mean to be a nosy neighbor, but Pamela just came home from school with a male friend. You remember we agreed we would keep an eye out for each other's kids. I hope this doesn't feel like I'm sticking my nose in where it doesn't belong." Dave assured me that he appreciated my call. About three minutes after we hung up, Pamela and her friend came walking past our house on the way back to school. There is a reason why teen pregnancy is low in our urban neighborhood.

The same kind of community involvement can lower the crime rate in a neighborhood. Our street abuts a public housing project. We share the same police precinct. But if you compare the police response time on Walker Avenue (our street) with that of Trestle Tree Apartments, you would discover a marked difference. Same police, same command leadership, but very different performance.

Walker Avenue has an active neighborhood association. It's more of a block club, really, that the 40 households have named Tapestry. The catalyst that initially pulled these families together was the need for a crime watch. Before we had a community name we had a common need—protection. Our area was plagued with crime, mostly break-ins and robberies by those who had to feed their drug habits.

One of our members, we discovered, had been with the military police in the Air Force and had some experience in law enforcement. His suggestion at our first community meeting was to invite the precinct commander to come and meet with us, give us tips on how to better protect ourselves, and tell us how to best support the work of the police who patrolled our street.

It turned out to be an excellent move. Not only did ranking police officers come to our meeting, but they also had some very practical tips on securing our homes and establishing a neighborhood watch. "If you see someone you don't know lingering on your street, call a neighbor so that two sets of eyes are on the stranger," they advised. "If he doesn't move on, ask him if he is looking for someone. If his answer isn't satisfactory, call us."

Undoubtedly, the most significant outcome of this meeting was the cooperative relationship that was established between the community and the police. Neighbors began waving to the patrol cars as they cruised down Walker Avenue. Information flowed back and forth about recent break-ins and car thefts and other incidents of concern. The day the Pearce home was burglarized really put the relationship to the test.

The Pearces were eating supper when a man climbed through their bedroom window, scooped all the jewelry and money he could find into Dave Pearce's brief case and slipped back out without being detected. Moments later the Pearces discovered the theft and immediately called the police.

Meanwhile, just down the street, another drama was playing out. Virgil Brown had just come out of his front door to bring his son's bicycle in for the night and discovered it missing. Irate that someone had stolen the nearly new bike, Virgil jumped into his neighbor's car since his was not running, and set out in search of the thief. A few blocks away he overtook a man peddling down the street on his son's bicycle carrying a briefcase. The man, startled at being discovered, dropped the bike and briefcase and took off running across side yards and down a back alley. Virgil picked up the abandoned booty and headed back to Walker Avenue.

As he rounded the corner to home, Virgil saw several police cars and a host of neighbors gathered in front of the Pearce house. Stopping to inquire, he was told that someone had broken into their home and made off with a briefcase full of valuables. "He stole my son's bike!" Virgil could hardly contain himself. "I have the stuff in my trunk. I saw the guy. I know where he is!"

Virgil led a convoy of the police cruisers to the spot where he had recovered the stolen merchandize and pointed them in the direction the thief had run. In a matter of moments police had the perpetrator in cuffs. They brought him back to the Pearces to see if anyone beside Virgil could make a positive identification. In spite of the man's threatening glares, several of the neighbors identified him as the one they had seen walking down the street with the briefcase. All said they would testify.

Three times neighbors took off work to appear as witnesses in court. And three times the perpetrator's lawyer requested continuances, a tactic designed to discourage witnesses and weaken the prosecution's case. Finally the judge said "no more" and the trial went forward. The man was convicted of the crime and is serving seven years. This incident cemented the relationship between the community and the police. Nothing is more demoralizing to the police than, after expending much effort to bring a predator to justice, to see him walk out of court with a smirk on his face because witnesses failed to show up.

This is one reason why the police response is so indifferent to the government-subsidized Trestle Tree Apartments. It is difficult to get straight stories there. People are afraid. Some will cover for known offenders because of family relationships or other entanglements. It's tough police work. But even when the police do manage to apprehend a perpetrator, it is very difficult to get witnesses to show up in court. Consequently, there is little motivation to "serve and protect." It's not right, but it is understandable. The key to a safe environment is not more police on the streets—the key is more effective community.

All this is not to say, of course, that programs and services are not needed in a community. On the contrary. The Boys' and Girls' Clubs, the city Parks and Recreation facilities, the Police Athletic Leagues—such programs that provide wholesome places and activities for residents serve to enhance the quality of life. Programs are important, but by themselves they are not sufficient.

The extent to which programs and services are run by those who live in the community will often be a measure of their effectiveness. If teachers live in the neighborhood where they teach and are known by the parents whose children they teach, they are far more likely to be involved in other aspects of their students' lives besides classroom performance. If police live in the apartment complex they are responsible to patrol, they will be far more aware of safety issues there than they would be in an area they view mostly from their cruiser window.

Being invested in one's community—and living there—yields the fruit of healthy self-interest. Initiatives owned by residents are likely to be more effective, personal, accountable and cost-effective than those funded and managed by outside professionals.

CHAPTER 16

COMMUNITY-FRIENDLY
PROGRAMS

An order of dedicated Catholic sisters in Cleveland had a wonderful problem. For more than a century, members of their order had ministered to the health needs of the poor of the city, growing a small examining room in a church into a multistate network of large modern hospitals. But times had changed since their modest beginnings. The government had taken over much of the responsibility for indigent healthcare, and a powerful new for-profit healthcare industry was buying the nonprofit medical centers.

It was a wrenching decision for the sisters to make, but modern realities brought them to consensus—they would sell their hospitals and reshape their ministry. Consequently, for the first time in their sacrificial history, they had more money than they needed to run their ministries. As I said, it was a wonderful problem.

I was invited to one of their discussions as they debated how best to invest their surplus resources. Their passion had always been to minister in the name of Christ to the dispossessed and marginalized, and they were committed to holding tight to that mission. Instead of owning and running all of the programs themselves, however, they decided to partner with other ministries that had expertise in various fields of service.

Treatment for the addicted was one of those areas they were concerned about. They had already made a substantial financial commitment to build and operate a drug treatment facility in an inner-city community that was plagued by drug abuse.

Two of their leaders drove me through the neighborhood to show me the site they had purchased. The architectural plans were impressive—a well-designed multistory professional building that would house up to 40 residents and accommodate more than four times that number of outpatients. They were obviously quite excited about the quality of both the facility and the program that would soon be serving this drug-infested neighborhood. It would fill a great need.

But I noticed as we drove around the area that a good number of large old Victorian-style homes had been renovated and that several new houses had been recently built. One whole block adjacent to the treatment center site was being developed with some very attractive middle-income houses. I asked who was buying these properties and was told that young professionals were moving back into the city. Property values were rising, my guides told me. They felt fortunate to have secured their property while prices were still depressed.

Something was wrong with the picture. These compassionate Christian ministers, committed to serving the poor of the city, were placing an institutional-style facility in the middle of a residential neighborhood that had every likelihood of rebounding with new economic and social life. Yes, there were presently many addicted people living in and around this community, and surely the need for treatment was dire.

But it would not be very long, a few short years at most, before the poor would be displaced by gentrification and the treatment center would be importing addicted people from other communities to fill its beds and counseling schedule. The last thing a neighborhood struggling to revive needs is a proliferation of human services that will ensure an ongoing flow of needy recipients into that community. One of the reasons a ghetto remains poor is because the need is so concentrated. If rebirth is to take place, a de-concentration of poverty and brokenness must take place. The community must become strong enough to deal internally with its own needs, needs that to treat and contain are in some manageable proportion to the capacity of the community.

It is understandable why ministries, agencies and institutions need to achieve certain economies of scale, why they must maintain enough traffic to justify the size of their budgets and buildings. A centralized approach to service certainly can improve efficiencies. And it is also quite predictable that institutions, both large and small, by their very nature become self-serving, even when their stated mission is to serve others. They quite quickly form systems and strategies that favor the interests of the institution over the people they serve and the communities where they are located. This is not a criticism—merely an observation of historical fact.

In light of these historical trends, I suggested to the sisters that they might want to consider a more community-friendly model of addressing the drug problem. Instead of building a commercial-style facility that would soon have to import addicted people into a residential neighborhood, they could buy a large old house or two, which would support the neighborhood restoration effort, and outfit it as a smaller-scale treatment center that would blend into the architectural character of the community.

When the need for treatment diminished in the immediate area, the facility could always be sold and become a family residence once again. Such an approach would give the sisters the flexibility to adapt to the changing urban landscape and to respond more rapidly to its shifting demographics. In this way they could at the same time serve the interests of the community as well as the needs of their target population.

But the train had already pulled out of the station. Their plans were drawn, their contracts negotiated, their methods set.

They would build their facility. I could hardly expect it to be different. After all, these Catholic sisters had a rich history of building institutions—hospitals to care for the sick and disenfranchised. Their mission had been fighting disease and restoring patients to health. And this mission could be accomplished effectively inside the walls of an institution.

The larger the institution, the more sick people they could cure. However, they had not viewed their mission through the eyes of the communities around them. If they had, they would have seen how ever-expanding institutions can sprawl over blocks of urban land, erecting parking decks where bungalows once stood, turning residential streets into busy thoroughfares. Had they considered their impact on the neighborhoods around them, they might have seen how institutional encroachment can discourage investment, choke a local economy and squeeze homeowners out. They might have seen how the healing of individuals can cause neighborhoods to become sick.

When we view health through a community development lens, our priorities shift. Economic vitality becomes equally important as physical vitality. Investments that strengthen the local economy, that attract new businesses back to the neighborhood and that cause housing values to appreciate—these are healthy community vital signs. On the other hand, investments that erode the basic building blocks of community (which are houses), that undermine local enterprise, that weaken the fabric of the neighborhood—such investments must be viewed as community-unfriendly.

Take the Parramore neighborhood of Orlando, for example. This inner-city community immediately adjacent to exploding downtown growth has been for years a blighted slum. The remaining homeowners of small bungalows were a few aging seniors; slumlords controlled the rest. It was here that many of the city's social services agencies clustered—homeless shelters, drug treatment programs, food banks, thrift stores, public agencies and so forth.

But Parramore is poised for new development. In-town development is hot on the market, and major corporations are assembling large and small parcels of land, while city planners are busily working on a dramatic new landscape. There is a commitment to ensure that existing residents retain a permanent, affordable place in the area, even as it is transformed into a mixed-income community. The vision for the resurgence of Parramore is stirring considerable excitement in Orlando.

The social service programs sense the excitement, too. For them it is a golden opportunity to piggyback on the heightened interest in Parramore and leverage that enthusiasm into new facilities and expanded programs. The area is still crime-ridden and poverty-stricken. There is still much redemptive work to be done there. And it can be done much more effectively in a modernized shelter, a new social service center, a state-of-the-art job training facility or a new Boys' and Girls' Club. Everyone wants to get in on the act. But there is a problem. The concentration of services for the poor that once made some sense in this area will not be needed here as the community revitalizes.

Whether for good or not, poor people and the problems that accompany poverty will be de-concentrated from Parramore, and new vested neighbors will infiltrate the community. If any new facility will be needed in the future, it will more likely be a health club rather than a homeless shelter.

As you might imagine, much controversy swirls around these issues. Real estate developers lobby for the highest density and upper-income limits that the market will bear. City planners argue for a balanced-income development that includes existing residents and attracts young professionals. Urban ministries prophetically cry out for the preservation of places for the most vulnerable. Politicians with moistened fingers in the air try to read the direction of the political winds of their constituencies. Each has a lens though which they are viewing Parramore. The lens of community development sees a healthy place for families, safe streets and parks where children can play, stores that serve the needs of neighbors, schools that educate, and attractive homes that appreciate. Rich or poor, these are common desires of families across the socioeconomic spectrum. Were a developer to view Parramore through a community lens, he might be more interested in a community park than his exclusive penthouse-level pool. Were an urban ministry to look through a community lens, it might be more interested in a quality grocery store than expanding their food bank warehouse. Everything depends on the vision.

Every community needs healthy institutions. Whether social, religious, educational, recreational, cultural, economic or governmental, institutions provide a society with stability and help preserve its quality of life. No community, however, can become or long remain vital if it is dominated by ever-expanding institutions that use up disproportionate amounts of its land at the expense of its residential fabric. A growing church that tears down houses to expand its parking capacity can find itself at cross-purposes with community health, even as a Catholic sisters' treatment center or an expanded homeless shelter can. Their community-friendliness depends largely upon the appropriateness of their scale.

CHAPTER 17

TRANSITION FROM PROGRAMS TO DEVELOPMENT

FCS Urban Ministries is an urban community development organization in Atlanta. It did not begin that way, however. Family Consultation Service was its original name—a nonprofit ministry created to provide counseling support to troubled adolescents and their families in Atlanta's inner city. Over time it grew into a multifaceted program that started businesses, built houses, provided healthcare, created schools and initiated a number of other needed services in the urban neighborhood it served.

Because a majority of staff lived in the community, the realities of neighborhood life influenced the shaping of the organization. As ministry leaders looked out of their living room windows at the daily streams of needy neighbors flowing in and out of a poorly stocked, overpriced corner grocery store, they were disturbed by the injustice. This eventually motivated them to get into the grocery business. Evicted families appearing at their front doors with nowhere to spend the night caused them to seek affordable housing options. Latchkey children who each year slipped further and further behind educationally moved them to initiate a preschool and then a K-8 elementary school. In time, the mission of FCS gravitated from a counseling ministry to a comprehensive community service organization.

Indeed, FCS did *serve* the community. But were they actually developing the community? No one could argue with the quali-

ty of their programs. Their jobs program enabled young people
(and parents) to enter the economic mainstream. Their housing program helped to move families out of public housing
into home ownership. But most of their "successes" meant that
these neighbors were leaving the community as the greener
fields of opportunity opened before them. What was good for
individuals was proving *not* good for the community. For example, FCS staff found themselves facilitating the out-migration
of some of their best neighbors. It was this realization that trig-
gered a complete reevaluation of FCS, not measured by how
well its clients were progressing but by how beneficial its services were to the strengthening of the community.

The results of the study were disconcerting. Much of the
service was *doing for* others, not *doing with* them and certainly not
enabling them to *do for themselves*. Their health clinic was a prime
example. Two physicians had combined their practices, which
freed them up to give full-time coverage to a clinic they established in the neighborhood. Their staff was caring and their
medical care was excellent. They helped to fill a widening gap of
uninsured patients.

The word of their affordable medical care soon spread well
beyond the community, eventually attracting people from more
than 75 miles away. This seemed to please the doctors since it
reflected well on the quality of their care. But when FCS leadership looked at health conditions in the immediate neighborhood, they found deficiencies of epidemic proportions. Pregnant
mothers were receiving virtually no prenatal care; nutritional deficiencies were resulting in a whole range of preventable illnesses;
seniors were often found to be isolated and malnourished.

The clinic was available for everyone—everyone who had the
initiative and capacity to access it, that is. But it had no outreach
strategy for actively promoting wellness, nor did its mission
include the organization of health watches, fairs, immunization

drives and other initiatives for the wellbeing of its community.

When it was suggested that lay healthcare volunteers be recruited and trained on every block to ensure that every pregnant mother came in for prenatal care, that every infant got immunized, that every homebound elder had someone looking out for their health needs, there was less-than-enthusiastic response. The doctors were quick to clarify that the mission of the clinic was treating illnesses, not community organizing. Combating disease was their primary orientation, not preventing sickness. And they certainly had no interest in a community health approach that diverted their energy from the examining room out into the homes and schools.

There was a similar response from the FCS school administrators. The preschool began as The Family Place. Its director lived within walking distance of the church where the preschool was located, and neighborhood residents were employed as teachers and aides. The majority of the students were from the immediate area, although a few (full-paying) students were dropped off by commuting parents.

Over time elementary grades were added and the school outgrew the church basement. A community center accommodated its growing enrollment, but by the addition of grade six a much larger facility was needed—a facility that was not to be found in the neighborhood. By this time the school (now called the Atlanta Youth Academy) was attracting students from all over the metropolitan area. Few came from the original neighborhood, so it made little difference where in the city the school was located.

Upon evaluating this program's impact on the neighborhood, it was found to have little to none. Its mission had moved from nurturing community children to providing a Christian education for the children of disadvantaged Atlanta families. This was certainly an important mission *but it was not community development.*

Program by program the evaluation proceeded, every ministry area being examined through the lens of community. Each program director was asked, How does your ministry strengthen the fabric of the community and enhance its capacity to become more self-sufficient? It was obvious that some programs would have to be restructured if they were to be more community-connected.

The youth ministry that had spread out (too thinly) to kids all over the city had to be refocused on the neighborhoods around the ministry center. The housing division limited its building and rehab activities to the immediate neighborhood. The ministry hired a local community organizer to establish block clubs, homeowner associations and crime watches. The Family Store (thrift store) developed a partnership with the local public school to both collect and provide affordable clothes for students and families. All FCS staff were encouraged to remain in or relocate into the community, thus seeding it with engaged and vested neighbor-leaders. The organization was clearly turning a corner. It was becoming a community development ministry in more than name only.

The most difficult part of retooling the community organization was deciding what to do with those good programs that were unwilling to adapt to a community development emphasis. The organization had come to a philosophical fork in the road that threatened to separate its family of ministries.

The health center was first to declare its position. They would not be changing their model. The doctors felt that they were providing a valuable service to a needy population and saw no reason to refocus their mission. This decision marked the beginning of a gradual (though amicable) separation that would lead to their independence from FCS. The school eventually followed suit. Although the relationships remained friendly and cooperative with both the health center and the school, both

formed separate 501(c)3 corporations and continued on their
original courses, serving families in need but not strengthening
the communities where they were located.

As FCS Urban Ministries continues to evolve into an in-
creasingly comprehensive community development organization, it has expanded its work to four additional inner-city
neighborhoods. The ministry only goes where it is invited by
community leadership and then only when there is a commitment to transformation, including spiritual, economic and
social dimensions.

They do not merely offer programs; they provide a total new
development strategy. Before making a commitment to partner
with a new neighborhood, they ask themselves the following
series of questions:

1. Is capable, indigenous (or indigenizing) visionary
   leadership behind the effort?
2. Is the plan neighborhood-specific? Does it focus on
   one and only one target community?
3. Is the effort comprehensive? Do the programmatic
   pieces all have as a primary objective the ultimate
   self-sufficiency of the neighborhood?
4. Does the plan emanate from local churches and/
   or people of faith? (People of faith are the greatest
   resource of hope and vision within any community.)
5. Does the plan protect against displacement or re-
   concentration of lower-income residents?
6. Does the plan promote inter-dependency rather than
   continued dependency?
7. Does the plan attract, retain and/or develop indigenous leadership in the community?
8. Does the plan attract new achieving neighbors into
   the community?

9. Does the plan utilize grants and nonprofits as catalysts for development that can eventually reduce the need for external subsidies?

10. Does the plan lead to economic neighborhood viability, as measured by its ability to attract and harness market forces?

Only if the answer to each question is yes and if they have available leadership to lead the mission will they move forward.

PART IV

FINAL THOUGHTS

It may have become obvious to the reader by this time that the changes this book points us toward will require skill sets and resources quite different from the counseling, social work talents typically found in the social service and ministry world.

Business acumen is needed if we are to transform our clothes closets into self-sustaining thrift stores. Real estate expertise will be required if we decide to shift from shelters to affordable housing alternatives. Those who know the drive it takes to build a profitable business are also very familiar with the goal-setting and no-nonsense management required to keep an operation growing. These marketplace gifts, often unappreciated by the softer sciences, are essential to the transformation suggested in the preceding pages. Thus, my parting words are directed specifically to those who make their living in the marketplace.

CHAPTER 18

TOWARD A THEOLOGY OF GENTRIFICATION

Building a new home in a run-down neighborhood in Atlanta was a decision that neither of our parents supported. It was a bad financial move, they counseled us, not to mention the danger. But my family was not relocating into the inner city for economic reasons. We had finally come to the conclusion that our ministry would be more effective if we lived among the people we felt called to serve than continue to commute from the suburbs. And so we graciously thanked our parents for their love and concern and went ahead with our construction plans.

New construction in the neighborhood was unheard of—at least for the 50 years prior to our arrival—and so the activity attracted much local attention. And some unexpected attention from outside real estate developers, as well. Within a few months of moving into our new home, we were delighted to see four new homes go up just two blocks from us, as well as a good number of renovations beginning throughout the neighborhood. Our property value was going to increase after all!

But during prayer and sharing times at our neighborhood church, we began to hear prayer requests for housing needs. "Please pray for us—our rents have just doubled." "Please pray for us—we've just gotten an eviction notice." It wasn't until Opal, a church member who lived within sight of the church, came in weeping one morning that I first made a disturbing connection. She had just received an eviction notice from the home she had lived in for many years—the city told the landlord to fix it up or board it up and he had decided to board it up until property values made it attractive to sell. For the first time it dawned on me that as my property value was nicely increasing, so was the price of the surrounding affordable homes. As my wealth was building, Opal's poverty was deepening. It was *my* investment that was the catalyst for her displacement. I could no longer sit in the circle and pray with integrity. I was the problem!

There was a name for this dilemma, I soon learned. Gentrification. It comes from the old English word "gentry," the land-rich ruling class of the sixteenth century who controlled the economy by virtue of their land holdings. "Landlords" they were called, the rulers of all who lived as tenants and laborers on their vast estates. They eventually disappeared from the social landscape with the emergence of the industrial revolution as wealth shifted away from the land and to the factories in burgeoning cities. The term "gentry" has been resurrected in our generation to describe the return of landowners to the city. I discovered that I was one of them. And it was not a compliment.

"Gentrification" by contemporary definition is "the restoration and upgrading of deteriorated urban property by the middle classes, often resulting in displacement of lower-income people." It is a new national norm. Over the past 50 years, American cities have declined as the suburbs have blossomed. This pattern is quite different from most of the large cities of the world where wealth and power are concentrated at the center and poverty spreads outward toward the outlying and less developed outskirts. In developing nations, people migrate from the rural areas, settle in poorer edge cities (or sometimes shantytowns outside the city) and try to work their way toward the prosperous center. U.S. cities, on the other hand, are like donuts with a hole in the middle and the dough around the outside. Our center cities are where our poverty is concentrated. But all this is changing. A massive demographic shift has begun, a great reversal as wealth returns to the inner core and poverty is pushed to the periphery. U.S. cities are beginning to conform to the pattern of most world cities, and in the process a diaspora—an uprooting and scattering—of the poor has begun.

I have now seen firsthand (yes, inadvertently participated in) the devastating impact that gentrification can have on the poor of an urban community. I have faced panicking families at my front door who had just been evicted from their homes, their meager belongings set out on the curb. I have helped them in their frantic search to find scarce affordable apartments and have collected donations to assist with rent and utility deposits.

But I have also seen what happens to the poor when the "gentry" *do not* return to the city. The effects of isolation are equally severe. Pathology creeps into a community when achieving neighbors depart—a disease born of isolation that depletes a work ethic, lowers aspirations and saps human initiative. I have seen courageous welfare mothers struggle in vain to save their children from the powerful undertow of the streets. I have witnessed the sinister forces of a drug culture as it ravages unchecked the lives of those who have few options for escape. Without the presence of strong, connected neighbor-leaders who have the best interests of the community at heart, a neglected neighborhood becomes a desperate dead-end place.

MUST GENTRIFICATION ALWAYS SPELL DISPLACEMENT FOR THE POOR?

The romantic notion that the culture of a dependent, poverty community must somehow be protected from the imposition of outside values is as naïve as it is destructive. Neighborhoods that have hemorrhaged for decades from the "up and out" migration of their best and brightest need far more than government grants, human services and urban ministries to restore their health. More than anything else, they need the return of the very kinds of home-owning, goal-driven, faith-motivated neighbors that once gave their community vitality. In a word, they need the gentry.

This leaves us in a bit of a quandary. The poor need the gentry in order to revive their deteriorated neighborhoods. But the gentry will inevitably displace the poor from these neighborhoods. The poor seem to get the short end of the stick either way.

But must gentrification always spell displacement for the poor? To some degree, yes. Yet displacement is not entirely bad. There are drug dealers and other rogues that *need* to be dislodged from a community if it is going to become a healthy place to raise children. Overcrowded tenements and flophouses *should* be thinned out or cleaned up, and this inevitably means displacement of some of the vulnerable along with their predators. Bringing responsible property management back into a neglected community does spell disruption for those who have chosen or been forced by necessity to endure slumlord economics. But what may be disruptive for the moment can become a blessing for those who yearn for a better way of life *if*—and this is a big *if*—the poor are included in the reclamation process by the returning gentry.

Opal forced me to look squarely into the face of this big *if.* Housing had not been on my radar screen when I moved into the city. It was not part of my ministry game plan. But neither could I sit passively in a prayer circle asking God to help my sister Opal knowing that my well-intentioned move was working to her detriment, knowing too that the same thing was about to happen over and over again to more of my church members and neighbors. And so I reordered my priorities. In addition to my church planting and mercy ministry strategy, I ventured into the arena of justice. I rallied suburban church partners to come to Opal's aid, bought and restored her house and structured a loan that enabled her to become a homeowner. Then, as my property value went up, so did hers. She became vested. Opal's house became for me a modern-day parable of "good news to the poor." Many of those who volunteered their time and skills to transform her home were deeply moved as they cared for a widow in this personal and practical way. They asked if there were other Opal's in our church. Indeed there were. The end result was the creation of a housing division within our ministry that has mobilized thousands of volunteers and enabled hundreds of Opals to become homeowners in our community.

GENTRIFICATION WITH JUSTICE

Gentrification with justice—that's what is needed to restore health to our urban neighborhoods. Needed are gentry with vision who have compassionate hearts as well as real estate acumen. We need gentry whose understanding of community includes the less advantaged, who will use their competencies and connections to ensure that their lower-income neighbors share a stake in their revitalizing neighborhood. The city needs landowning residents who are also faith-motivated, who yield to the tenets of their faith in the inevitable tension between values of neighbor over values of property. That is why gentrification needs a theology to guide it.

The people of the Kingdom have a unique mandate to care for the needs of the vulnerable and the voiceless. Our Scriptures are quite clear about this. It has been from antiquity both our birthright and our responsibility. We cannot rightly take joy in the rebirth of the city if no provision is being made to include the poor as co-participants. It will not be enough to offer food baskets at Christmas to migrating masses of needy people who are being driven by market forces away from the vital services of the city. Nor will our well-intentioned programs and ministries suffice for those being scattered to unwelcoming edge cities. We must be more intelligent than this. More strategic.

While we remain committed to fulfilling the Great Commission, there is a prior command to which the followers of Christ are called. The Great Command, loving God, and its inseparable companion, loving neighbor, form the bedrock of our faith. All the Law and Prophets are built upon this foundation, our Lord said. The prophet Micah captured its essence: He has told you, oh man, what is good and what the Lord desires of you, that you do justice and love mercy and walk humbly with your God (see Mic. 6:8).

The Body of Christ is amply resourced with the very talents needed to bring about both mercy and justice in our changing cities. In addition to those more spiritual sounding gifts—those we have heard sermons about—there is a vast untapped reservoir of giftedness ready to channel into the work of the Kingdom—secular sounding gifts like deal-making, lending, insuring, lawyering, marketing, architecture, and real estate developing, to name but a few. Under the Lordship of Christ, these become spiritual gifts ideally designed for the work of biblical justice.

The "Christ-ones" who believe that their highest calling is to love God and love their neighbor are the very ones equipped to infuse into our culture both values and actions that will have redemptive outcomes. We can buy crack houses and renovate them into residences for mission-minded couples. We can structure deals to develop mixed-income housing. We can create innovative housing policies that will induce developers to include lower-income residents in their plans. We can pass ordinances that will give tax relief to seniors on fixed incomes so that they can remain in their homes. We can establish loan funds to give down-payment assistance to lower-income homebuyers. If we are both caring *and thinking* people, we can use our influence and resources to develop the means by which the least of these can share in the benefits of a reviving city—and foster healthy growth at the same time. We can harness the growing tide of gentrification so that it becomes a redemptive force in our cities. In a word, we can bring about gentrification with justice.

NEW MINISTRY PARADIGMS

Resisting gentrification is like trying to hold back the rising ocean tide. It is surely coming, relentlessly, with power and growing momentum. Young professionals as well as empty nesters are flooding into our cities, buying up lofts and condos and dilapidated historic residences, opening avant-garde artist studios and gourmet eateries. If market forces alone are allowed to rule the day, the poor will be gradually, silently displaced, for the market has no conscience. But those who do understand God's heart for the poor have a historic challenge to infuse the values of compassion and justice into the process. But it will require altogether new paradigms of ministry.

The inner-city church that is committed to reaching out to meet the needs of its immediate parish will soon be confronted with the disappearance of lower-income neighbors. Such urban ministries are approaching an inevitable T in the road. If they remain committed to the poor, they must decide to either follow the migration streams as they gravitate to the periphery of the city, or get involved in real estate to capture affordable property in their neighborhood to ensure that their low-income neighbors retain a permanent place. Migrant ministries move with the people, establish ministry centers in the affordable suburban apartments and remain flexible. Community development ministries, on the other hand, remain rooted in the parish, purchase housing and land, and form partnerships with builders and developers that enable their members (neighbors) to remain in a reviving community that has a healthy mix of incomes. Either strategy is legitimate. Both require significant retooling.

Gentrification brings to the suburban Church an altogether different challenge. The poor are now showing up in the classrooms and bus stops and grocery stores of homogenous neighborhoods once thought to be safely beyond the reach of inner-city troubles. Mission-minded churches that for years have been journeying down to the ghetto to serve those in need now find these needs at their own doorstep. The new hues, the unfamiliar languages, the unintelligible signs on new businesses in the strip malls—these are the sure indicators that gentrification is reaching the suburbs. They also signal a new era of opportunity for the suburban Church. It is a divine invitation to the Church to extend a welcoming hand, to start new congregations, to share facilities, to hire new workers, to teach ESL classes, to acquire and manage housing that ensures a hospitable environment. It is a unique time in history to "let your light so shine before men [in your neighborhood] that they may see your good works and glorify your Father in heaven" (Matt. 5:16).

A FEW GUIDING PRINCIPLES

The definitive works have yet to be written on how to harness gentrification for the purposes of the Kingdom. However, a few guiding principles are rising to the surface from some of the best practices around the country. Here are just a few.

Gentrification is our new reality. Some rail against it; others laud its arrival. But for good or ill, it is our new reality, and it will only increase in the years to come. Gentrification means to welcome a new economic and social life for our cities and, with the proactive involvement of the saints, can introduce a whole new era of hopefulness for the poor. Our mantra must be: gentrification with justice.

Diversity is a gift. Communities that are economically and racially mixed can be the richest of environments for families as well as singles and older adults. Diverse community is God's plan, the final destination toward which all the righteous are heading—the City of our God where people of every tribe, every nation and every tongue will take up eternal residence.

Community doesn't just happen. Especially not diverse community. It must be built. Focused and sustained effort must be invested in getting to know neighbors, organizing community activities, modeling neighborliness and communicating good news. Love of neighbor must be practical and visible over time.

Indigenous neighbors are a treasure. It is easy to ignore seniors, easy to push on past less communicative neighbors, easy to exclude those who don't show up at community functions. But the rich history of the neighborhood is imbedded in the lives and family albums of long-term residents. The effort to extract and honor this history is well worth the time and effort. And everyone, no matter how unlikely, has some valuable talent to contribute to the life of the community.

Economic viability is essential. A community will not be healthy unless it has ample neighbors with discretionary income to attract and sustain businesses. The gentry are essential. However, justice demands that we ensure that the poor are embraced and included as beneficiaries in a healthy community.

God's shalom must be worked at. The roles of peacemakers, communicators, gatherers, organizers and connectors are some of the most vital talents needed for the establishment of peace and prosperity and a prevailing sense of well-being that God desires for His creation. Shalom is not merely the absence of crime on the street, but it is also the prevailing presence of peace and goodness in the relationships of God's diverse family. It is achieved only by intentional effort.

CHAPTER 19

A GIFT FIT FOR A KING

Nobody loves to turn a deal like a businessperson. I love to watch them congregate at restaurants, salivating more over a savory sale than their scrumptious steak. Some lean forward in undistracted intensity. Others spin humorous anecdotes designed to soften the heart as well as sales resistance. Some use warmth and charm, while others cut brusquely through the fluff to the bottom line. It's a wonderful choreography of cunning and competition.

What is amazing, of course, is that these wheeler-dealers end up accomplishing astonishing feats: They build skyscrapers, start banks and conceptualize never-before-thought-of products. For you who love to turn your talents in the marketplace, I have some great news!

The Christ who was born in poverty got His initial start-up capital from three wealthy businessmen. Successful and educated, these men (wise, they were called) had economic and political independence that allowed them to study religion, travel internationally and engage in foreign investments. They researched Hebrew tradition, used their political savvy to locate the Jewish boy king and then made personal contact with Him.

The good news is that their gifts—their commerce-generated wealth—became sacred in the process. Something new happened in their transaction with the Christ child: Their medium of economic exchange (gold) was sanctified. Filthy lucre became purified. And symbols of extravagance (frankincense and myrrh) became expressions of the Divine.

Good news, you who are wise in the ways of the world. The line between the secular and sacred has been erased. The profane is made holy. You realize what this means, don't you? The ability to build a business is equal with the ability to preach a sermon. The skill of salesmanship has equal value with that of administering sacraments. Every talent or treasure offered to the Christ becomes sacred. There is no such thing as a nonspiritual gift—only a nonspiritual motivation that sometimes contaminates a giver.

The bottom line is this: The gift most valued by the Christ is the one most valued by you. The talents you enjoy most—those vision-casting, deal-making, product-promoting talents that churn up energy within you—those are the very gifts needed in the work of Christ's kingdom.

Your real estate expertise is a gift as precious as gold when presented to the homeless Christ. And with your architectural talents, you may design for Him a home. For His brothers and sisters (the least of these), you may bring your gifts of merchandising and marketing and design economic innovations to feed and clothe them with dignity. You are invited to bring your most valuable assets—your talent, experience and connections—to create for the Christ a whole new technology of compassion.

Don't reach for your billfold; it is not close enough to your heart. Don't raise your hand to volunteer for another committee in the ecclesiastical bureaucracy; tokenism is an unfit gift. Rather, look within. What invigorates you? What causes you to wake up before dawn with a new idea spinning in your mind? What fuels your imagination, even when you are fatigued? Here is where you will find your most valued treasure. Here is where you will find a gift worthy of your Lord.

THE EIGHT COMPONENTS OF CHRISTIAN COMMUNITY DEVELOPMENT

Dr. Wayne L. Gordon
CCDA Chairman

Nehemiah begins with lamenting over the city of Jerusalem: "Those who survived the exile and are back in the province are in great trouble and disgrace. The wall of Jerusalem is broken down, and its gates have been burned with fire" (Neh. 1:3, *NIV*).

This describes the situation in parts of most American cities today. They have been neglected and allowed to deteriorate for almost 40 years. The Church of Jesus Christ has at best sat back and watched this happen, yet in many areas has contributed to the problem. The words of Nehemiah, "great trouble and disgrace," ring true for us in the Church today.

The question arises as to what the response of Christians will be to the troubles of the poor and the inner cities today. The desperate conditions that face the poor call for a revolution in the Church's attempts at a solution. Through years of experience among the poor, many have come to see that these desperate problems cannot be solved without strong commitment, heroic faith and risky actions on the parts of ordinary Christians.

There are many philosophies that seek to solve the problems of the poor, but most fall short of any lasting change. The most creative long-term solutions to the problems of the poor are coming from grass-roots and church-based efforts. The solutions are coming from people who see themselves as the replacements, the agents, for Jesus here on Earth, in their own neighborhoods and communities.

Those who see themselves as Christ's agents have formed a philosophy that is known as Christian Community Development. This philosophy is not a concept developed in a classroom, nor is it formulated by people foreign to the poor community. These are biblical, practical principles evolved from years of living and working among the poor.

John Perkins, in Mississippi, first developed this philosophy. John and Vera Mae Perkins moved back to their homeland of Mississippi from California in 1960 to help alleviate poverty and oppression. Through their work and ministry, Christian Community Development was conceived. Christian Community Development has a proven track record with over 600 models around the country that are making great progress in difficult communities.

THE EIGHT COMPONENTS

Christian Community Development has eight essential components that have evolved over the last 40 years. The first three are based on John Perkins's Three *Rs* of community development: relocation, reconciliation and redistribution. The rest have been developed by many Christians who are working together to find ways to rebuild poor neighborhoods. The following is a brief description of the eight key components to Christian Community Development.

Relocation: Living Among the People

Living out the gospel means desiring the same thing for your neighbor and neighbor's family as that which you desire for yourself and your family. Living out the gospel means bettering the quality of other people's lives spiritually, physically, socially and emotionally as you better your own life. Living out the gospel means sharing in the suffering and pain of others.

A key phrase to understanding relocation is "incarnational ministry." How did Jesus love? "The Word became flesh and dwelt among us, and we beheld His glory, the glory as of the only begotten of the Father, full of grace and truth" (John 1:14). Jesus relocated. He became one of us. He didn't commute back and forth to heaven. Similarly, the most effective messenger of the gospel to the poor will also live among those to whom God has called that person.

Relocation is community-based in the very essence of the word. There are three kinds of people who live in the community. First, "relocators" are people who were not born in the inner city but moved into the neighborhood. Second are the "returners." These are the people born and raised in their community who then left for a better life. Usually they return from college or the military. They are no longer trapped by the surrounding poverty of their neighborhood. Yet, they choose to return and live in the community they once tried to escape. Last are the "remainers." These are the ones that could have fled the problems of the inner city but chose to stay and be part of the solution to the problems surrounding them.

By relocating, a person will understand most clearly the real problems facing the poor and then he or she may begin to look for real solutions. For example, if a person ministering in a poor community has children, one can be sure that person will do everything possible to ensure that the children of the community get a good education. Relocation transforms "you, them and theirs" to "we, us and ours." Effective ministries plant and build communities of believers that have a personal stake in the development of their neighborhoods.

There is no question that relocation is the linchpin of Christian Community Development and that all other principles of development draw on it for meaning.

Reconciliation

Reconciling People to God. Reconciliation is at the heart of the gospel.
Jesus said that the essence of Christianity could be summed up
in two inseparable commandments: Love God and love thy neighbor (see Matt. 22:37-39). First, then, Christian Community Development is concerned with reconciling people to God and
bringing them into a church fellowship where they can be disci-
pled in their faith.

Evangelism is very much a part of Christian Community
Development. The answer to community development is not
just providing a job or a decent place to live, but it is also having a true relationship with Jesus Christ. It is essential that the
good news of Jesus Christ is proclaimed and that individuals
place their faith in Him for salvation.

The gospel, rightly understood, is "wholistic." It responds to
people as whole people; it does not single out just spiritual or
just physical needs and speak to those. Christian Community
Development begins with people being transformed by the love
of God, who then respond to God's call to share the gospel
with others through evangelism, social action, economic development and justice.

Reconciling People to People. The most racially segregated time
of the week in our nation is Sunday morning during church
services. At church, Christians often pray the model prayer that
the Lord taught: "Your kingdom come, your will be done on
earth as it is in heaven" (Matt. 6:10, *NIV*). This prayer teaches that
churches should reflect heaven on Earth—and heaven will be the
most integrated place in the world. People of every nation and
every tongue will worship Christ together. This is the picture of
the Church that Christ presents to His people. American churches, however, are rarely integrated and thus weaken the gospel
because of this practice.

The question that we're left with, then, is, Can a gospel that reconciles people to God without reconciling people to people be the true gospel of Jesus Christ? A person's love for Christ should break down every racial, ethnic and economic barrier in a united effort to solve the problems of the community. For example, Christian Community Development recognizes that the entire Body of Christ—black, white, brown and yellow; rich and poor; urban and suburban; educated and uneducated—needs to share the task of loving the poor.

While the Bible transcends culture and race, the Church is still having a hard time with living out the reality of unity in Christ. Christian Community Development, on the other hand, is intentional about reconciliation and works hard to bring people of all races and cultures into the one worshiping Body of Christ. This comes not so much through a program but through a commitment to living together in the same neighborhood. This is why relocation is so important.

This is also where what Dr. John Perkins calls the *felt-need concept* can be so helpful for individuals who are seeking to establish authentic cross-cultural relationships in under-resourced neighborhoods. In order to build trust with people who may be suspicious about our motives for being in the "hood" because of negative past experiences, stereotypes or ignorance, we must begin by getting to know people right where they are. As we listen to their stories and get to know their hopes and concerns for the present and future, we also begin to identify the community's deepest felt-needs: those hurts and longings that allow us opportunities to connect with people on a deeper level, which is always necessary for true reconciliation to take place.

The power of authentic reconciliation between God and us, and between people of every culture and race is an essential component of effective ministry in our hurting world.

Redistribution (Just Distribution of Resources)

When men and women in the Body of Christ are visibly present and living among the poor (relocation), and when people are intentionally loving their neighbors and their neighbors' families as their own (reconciliation), the result is redistribution, or a just distribution of resources. When God's people who have resources (regardless of their race or culture) commit to living in underserved communities, seeking to be good neighbors, being examples of what it means to be a follower of Christ, working for justice for the entire community, and utilizing their skills and resources to address the problems of that community alongside their neighbors, then redistribution is being practiced.

Redistribution brings the principles of justice back to the underserved communities. Justice has left communities of color and lower economic status, leaving an unjust criminal court and prison system, unjust hiring practices, unjust housing development, and injustice in the educational institutions. Justice has been available only to people with the economic means to acquire just treatment.

Redistribution, though, brings new skills, new relationships and new resources and puts them to work to empower the residents of a given community to bring about healthy transformation. This is redistribution: when Christian Community Development ministries harness the commitment and energy of men, women and young people living in the community, and others who care about their community, and find creative avenues to develop jobs, schools, health centers, home ownership opportunities and other enterprises of long-term development.

Seeking a just distribution of resources and working for justice in underserved communities contribute greatly to helping people help themselves, which is at the heart of Christian Community Development.

Leadership Development

The primary goal of leadership development is to develop leaders in order to restore the stabilizing glue and fill the vacuum of moral, spiritual and economic leadership that is so prevalent in poor communities. This is accomplished most effectively by raising up Christian leaders from the community of need who will remain in the community to live and lead. Most Christian Community Development ministries put a major focus on youth development, winning youth to Christ as early as kindergarten and then following them all the way through college with spiritual and educational nurturing. Upon returning to the community from college, a ministry creates opportunities for those former students to exercise leadership.

At the core of the leadership vacuum in inner-city communities is an attitude of flight. For many, success is defined as being able to move out of inner-city communities, to own a home in a more affluent area. The erroneous goal is to help a few people leave the neighborhood so that they can escape the problems of inner-city communities. But this core value of escapism has caused a major drain on inner-city communities.

There is a drain on leadership development because it is possible only when there is longevity of ministry. All too often people are guilty of trying to have quick fixes in poor neighborhoods. For example, since leadership development is of the highest priority in Christian Community Development, each ministry must have a dynamic youth ministry. And each youth ministry must be reaching young people with the good news of Jesus Christ and then equipping them to become faithful followers of Christ and effective community leaders. This will take at least 15 years to accomplish, so a worker must plan to stay in the neighborhood for at least that long.

In situations where Latinos and other ethnic groups are negatively affected by their current legal status in our country, this progressive, developmental process is nearly impossible to accomplish, as young people are not able to attend college or prepare for a stable career. In this case, ministries are often moved to engage in social action to challenge and change current immigration laws that debilitate the lives of promising youths and their families.

For CCD ministries, developing leaders from the community is a huge priority that requires absolute commitment. The payoff is that our communities will be filled with strong Christian leaders who love their neighbors and have the skills and abilities to lead our churches, organizations and other institutions to bring sustainable health to our communities.

Listening to Community

Often communities are developed by people from the outside who bring in resources without taking into account the community itself. Christian Community Development, however, is committed to listening to the community residents and hearing their dreams, ideas and thoughts. This is often referred to as the *felt need concept*. Listening is most important, as the people of the community are the vested treasures of the future.

It is important not to focus on the weaknesses or needs of a community. Again, the felt need concept, as referred to above, helps us as community developers to focus on the desires of the community residents. The priority is the thoughts and dreams of the community itself—what the people themselves believe should be the focus. Asset-based community development focuses on the assets of a community and builds upon them. When felt needs are fused together with community assets through Christian Community Development, this can have extremely positive results.

Every community has assets that are often neglected. When a ministry utilizes *Asset-Based Community Development* (ABCD), it names all of the assets in the community that help the community see its many positive characteristics. It is through these assets that people develop their community.

Christian Community Development realistically points out, through community meetings and efforts, some of the areas that people in the community would like to see improved. The areas to be focused on are not looked at from some outside group or demographic study that is laid upon the community. Instead, it is the community members themselves who decide what areas they would like to improve.

After a community has decided where it wants to focus some of its attention, it is then directed to the means with which it can bring this about. What qualities, talents and abilities does the community have that can help solve these problems? The focus is on the community members seeing themselves as the solution to the problem, not some government program or outside group that is going to be their salvation.

It is essential for community leaders to help the community focus on maximizing their strengths and abilities to make a difference for their community. The philosophy of Christian Community Development believes that the people with the problems have the best solutions and opportunities to solve those problems. Christian Community Development, then, affirms the dignity of individuals and encourages the engagement of the community to use its own resources and assets to bring about sustainable change.

Church-based Community Development

Nothing other than the community of God's people is capable of affirming the dignity of the poor and enabling them to meet their own needs. It is practically impossible to do effective wholistic ministry apart from the local church. A nurturing community of faith can best provide the thrusts of evangelism,

discipleship, spiritual accountability and relationships by
which disciples grow in their walk with God.

One problem today, however, has been that the Church is
not involved in developing its communities. Often, the Church
has been an unfriendly neighbor in communities across our
country. Churches are guilty of being open only on Sunday
mornings and Wednesday nights and being almost irrelevant
to the needs of the people around them. Because of this, many
parachurch organizations have started to do the work of loving
their neighbors that the Church has neglected.

Christian Community Development, in contrast, sees the
Church as taking action toward the development of its community. It is the responsibility of the Church to evangelize, disciple
and nurture people in the Kingdom. Yet, from the command of
Jesus, it is also the responsibility of the Church to love their
neighbor and their neighborhood. Churches, then, should be
seen as lovers of their communities and neighborhoods.

As community and neighborhood lovers, it is out of the
Church body that ideas and programs that bolster community
life should emerge. This concept is certainly not new in the
black community. The black Church has spawned most of
the substantial community efforts in housing and economic
development. There have been shopping centers built, senior
housing units developed and communities transformed by
the Church. As natural as these transformations have been for
the black Church (also, recently many new efforts are emerging in
the Latino and Asian communities that are making the Church
even more relevant to those they serve), they continue to be foreign to the traditional white Church. Often, opposition to the
Church's involvement in community development still occurs
among many white denominations and Church groups.

Finally, probably the greatest sustaining power of community development is the presence of a local church. Because

Christian Community Development is based on relocation and people living in the community, having a local church in which to worship together is essential. It is in the church where people gather to be rejuvenated and have their personal needs met. This is true of staff members and non-staff members. How exciting it is to see doctors at a local health center worshiping and sitting next to their patients on a Sunday morning. This is community building at its best.

The church helps people to understand that each person has gifts and talents and that all must utilize those for the greater good of the community. And a worshiping church breaks down many of the barriers, including racial, educational and cultural barriers, that often separate people in communities.

A Wholistic Approach

Often, many in ministry get passionate and involved in one area of need and think that if they solve that one particular problem that all else will be resolved. Christians, of course, often focus this area on a personal relationship with Jesus Christ. Certainly, the most essential elements to Christian Community Development are evangelism and discipleship. Yet solving problems with lasting solutions requires more.

There is never a simplistic answer to the problems in poor communities. Often, people will say that the problem is spiritual, social or educational. These are problems, but they are only part of the larger problems. Solving the housing problem does not solve the emotional struggles that a person has. Christian Community Development, though, has a wholistic approach to ministry that deals with the spiritual, social, economic, political, cultural, emotional, physical, moral, judicial, educational and familial issues of each person.

The wholistic approach is difficult because there are so many aspects to a person's life. That is why there is no better way of helping a person than having him or her committed to a local church. A church that is committed to Christian Community Development sees not only the soul of a person as significant but also his or her whole life on Earth. It is being completely pro-life for a person, not only eternally, but also as the person lives on this earth.

Therefore, Christian Community Development sees that the Church must be involved in every aspect of a person's life. In order to accomplish the wholistic aspect of ministry, pastors and leaders must be networkers. Christian Community Development builds coalitions in communities so that they can work together to solve the problems.

Empowerment

Empowering people as community developers to meet their needs is an important element to Christian Community Development. How does a pastor ensure that people are able to help themselves after they have been helped? Often Christian ministry, particularly in poor communities, creates dependency. This is no better than the federal government welfare program. But the Bible teaches empowerment, not dependency.

In the Old Testament, empowerment is an important aspect to God's care for the poor. In Deuteronomy 24 and Leviticus 19, God instituted the gleaning system. The farmers harvested their crops but were only allowed to go through the field one time. What was left behind or dropped on the ground was available for any widow, alien, orphan or poor person to come and harvest. Thus, this program was one that empowered people.

Three principles come out of God's welfare system in the Old Testament. First, there must be opportunity for people to get their needs met. In Deuteronomy and Leviticus, this happened to be a field with food in it. Second, the person who has a need must be willing to work for it. The widow, alien, orphan or poor person had to go into the field and pick up the crops which, then, involved work on the part of the poor. This is also found in 2 Thessalonians 3:10, which says that if you don't work, you don't eat. Third, when these first two principles are working, a person's dignity is affirmed. All people have inherited dignity because we were all created in the image of God. Oftentimes, charity demeans a person and strips him or her of dignity. In contrast, the last principle of empowerment affirms a person's God-given dignity.

TRACK RECORD

There are over 600 organizations in over 200 cities and 40 states practicing Christian Community Development. These churches and ministries are showing that it is possible that the Church can live out the love of God in the world; that black and white and yellow and brown, rich and poor together, can be reconciled; that we can make a difference; that we can rescue the ghettoes and barrios of this nation.

In these hundreds of communities and cities across the world, these defining principles of Christian Community Development are proving that grass-roots, community-based ministries led by people who have made the community their own are the most effective agents for healing the poor.

The following poem is used as a philosophical guide to those working on Christian Community Development:

Go to the people
Live among them
Learn from them
Love them
Start with what they know
Build on what they have:

But of the best leaders
When their task is done
The people will remark
"We have done it ourselves."

CONCLUSION

Clearly there are great needs in neglected inner-city communities throughout our nation. There is a lack of leadership in these communities, and it is essential that new leadership be developed from among the people. These communities face a variety of cultural and environmental factors that impact the health of these neighborhoods. Thus, Christian Community Development, I believe, represents the best approach to not only develop these future leaders but also to transform our most under-resourced communities into thriving communities through the power of God and the efforts of His people.

ABOUT THE AUTHOR

Bob Lupton has invested the last 34 years in inner-city Atlanta, Georgia. In response to a call that he first felt while serving in Vietnam, he left a budding business career to work with delinquent urban youth. His life's work has been the rebuilding of urban neighborhoods where families can flourish and children can grow into healthy adults.

Bob is a Christian community developer and an entrepreneur who brings together communities of resource with communities of need. Through FCS Urban Ministries—a nonprofit organization he founded—he has developed three mixed-income subdivisions, organized two multiracial congregations, started a number of businesses, created housing for hundreds of families, and initiated a wide range of human services in his community.

He is the author of the books *Theirs Is the Kingdom, Return Flight* and the widely circulated *Urban Perspectives—Reflections from the Gospel, Grace and the City*. Bob has a PhD in psychology from the University of Georgia. He serves as a speaker, strategist and inspirer with and for those who seek to establish God's Shalom in the city.

ABOUT THE CCDA INSTITUTE

This book is presented by the Christian Community Development Association (CCDA) as a practical tool for assisting ministries to enhance their effectiveness in community building. CCDA is a supportive network of urban practitioners, educators and churches committed to the work of God's kingdom, especially as it relates to compassion and justice for the poor.

A driving force behind the growth and influence of the Christian Community Development movement has been the writing of our founder, Dr. John Perkins. Throughout the country and around the world, there are hundreds of ministries that have been born as a result of someone reading one of John's books, among them: *Let Justice Roll Down, Justice for All* and *Beyond Charity*.

Along with the impact of Dr. Perkins's books have been training events or conferences where Dr. Perkins and other CCD leaders have taught the eight key components of CCD.

After many years of seeing the need for a more formalized way to disseminate the philosophy and heart of Christian Community Development, in late 2004, the Christian Community Development Association launched the CCDA Institute to offer regional training for our members and to introduce others engaged in urban ministry or community development to our unique philosophy based on the eight key components of CCD:

- Relocation: The Theology and Practice of Incarnational Ministry
- Reconciliation in the New Millennium
- Redistribution: Toward a Just Distribution of Resources
- Listening to the Community
- Indigenous Leadership Development

- Church-based Community Development
- Empowerment: Moving from Betterment to Empowerment
- Wholistic Ministry: Reaching the Whole Person with the Whole Gospel

The delivery of high caliber training for emerging leaders and the production of books, curriculum, Web-based resources and other training materials is of utmost importance if CCDA is going to accomplish our vision and mission.

The mission of CCDA is to inspire and train Christians who seek to bear witness to the kingdom of God by reclaiming and restoring under-resourced communities. The vision of CCDA is to have wholistically restored communities with Christians fully engaged in the process of transformation.

With the publication of this book by Dr. Robert Lupton, and through his writing, we are excited to offer our first CCDA Institute publication. Our desire is that *Compassion, Justice and the Christian Life* will challenge and inspire both you and the Church to, as our mission says, "fully engage in the process of transforming under-resourced communities."

For information regarding membership, events and other resources available through CCDA, or to find out how to earn a certificate degree from CCDA in Christian Community Development, please visit our website (www.ccda.org) or contact us at:

Christian Community Development Association
3555 W. Ogden Avenue
Chicago, IL 60623

Website: www.CCDA.org
Phone: 773-762-0994